Thanks Doctor...

BY ROBERT D. CARPENTER. M.D.

Published by RDC Publishers
P.O. Box 1817, Whittier, California 90609

ISBN 0-9600576-1-7
Library of Congress Catalog Card No 72-78231

To my three loves:
God, family and patients

FOREWORD

I first met Robert Carpenter as an undergraduate student at Wheaton College in the 1940's. Becoming his friend was easy, because Bob knows no stranger. He was a good student, involved in many campus activities, and fully dedicated to a life of service.

His broad experience in the three decades of his involvement with medicine has prepared him well for the writing of this book. I recall vividly my first discussion with Bob as he excitedly described this editorial undertaking. He related to me his experience in medical missionary work in Africa and his establishing of a medical practice in Southern California. In addition to his practice, he serves as medical consultant for the special educational programs in five school districts, working with children from kindergarten through high school. This broad background and his realistic medical approach to the problems of learning made him the logical choice to address a gathering of some 150 teachers of handicapped children in the Garden Grove Unified School District where I serve as superintendent. This school district—eighth largest in the entire state—has the largest program of handicapped and multihandicapped children in Orange County, the second largest in the State of California, and one of its most rapidly expanding counties.

The response to Dr. Carpenter's approach to learning by those teachers and administrators was favorable. They recognized at once his enthusiasm and practical suggestions for helping youngsters and for understanding their problems.

Many parents today are desperately seeking to help their children in the complicated learning process. They too often seek to attack only the individual problem at hand when it is the *whole child* who needs help. Dr. Carpenter calls for "total vision, not tunnel vision" in today's society. He is deeply dedicated to assisting children and has the expertise to assist also their parents and teachers, seeking to help the child to attain success in the learning process.

The author has taken many hours from his successful practice to prepare this book which is based on up-to-date information and his personal experience with children, young people and adults. His medical practice as a missionary in Africa, as well as his personal service to a total of eight public school districts in Southern California, bring a wealth of personal and professional experience to this presentation. *Thanks Doctor* is "must" reading for the educator and the parent. Both can gain understanding in the common effort of home and school to help children learn.

During my past 26 years of teaching, from elementary to college classrooms (including 20 years in school administration), I have read many books and articles in the field of education. I have examined and read books dealing with the learner and the learning process, each book adding to a basic knowledge of learning. But this volume is unique because it presents to the reader the "whole pupil" concept. This approach to an important problem of society—the teaching of the young—brings into perspective man's relationship to himself and to God.

Dr. Carpenter's personal commitment to serving God and man is evident in his writing. His fresh approach to many of the problems facing the parent and the teacher fires the reader with zeal for employing new and effective solutions in learning disabilities. The reader will recognize through the pages of this book that there is after all a way of teaching the young, regardless of the handicap and of the difficulties encountered.

David H. Paynter, Ed. D.
Superintendent

Garden Grove Unified School District
Garden Grove, California

AUTHOR'S PREFACE

No one can change the past, therefore the record of each person's life must stand as it has been lived.

Whether that record is filled with noble or ignoble pursuits was determined by the smallest details in the early beginnings of study and learning. The blame for a life of failure can often be laid simply to underachievement in elementary education.

In search of remedies, the teacher concentrates on improving teaching techniques and on helping students to improve their poor attitudes in the classroom; the psychologist prescribes counsel; the sociologist recommends more adequate relationships. Undoubtedly any one or a combination of these factors has contributed to helping children with learning problems.

This book boldly outlines a new concept, adding another dimension to traditional methods of treatment for underachievers. The main purpose is to present a total view of the cause, diagnosis and treatment of learning disabilities among children. It will also explore associated behavioral problems from the viewpoint of medical, psychological, sociological and educational disciplines. This total view is based on an integrated cooperative system which is presently functioning in several Southern California school districts* and in the author's private practice. At the center of all considerations will be the "whole-person" principle involving the child's physical, psychological and spiritual makeup.

Parents, nurses, doctors and all educational specialists will find in this presentation a variety of possible courses of action available to help the child with learning problems. The book seeks to present a total view showing a clearer picture of the various interrelated parts. Most of these parts are specialties or sub-specialties in their own right.

---

*Baldwin Park Unified School District, La Puente-Hacienda Unified School District, Little Lake City School District, Los Nietos School District, Rowland Unified School District, San Gabriel School District, South Whittier School District, and Whittier Union High School District.

The rapid accumulation of information in various related fields makes it impossible for one person to keep current on all innovations. Therefore this volume highlights the latest research and offers further information for those desiring to study them in detail.

Learning disabilities vary greatly among students. What helps one child will not necessarily help another, even though the problems are similar. Therefore a broader view aids both in the diagnosis and in the treatment, allowing students to progress further at their individual rate.

Most educators and school psychologists are aware to some degree of the special educational and psychological methods that can be employed to aid students with learning problems. Some know, for example, that proper medication can calm the over-active child and cause a dramatic improvement in behavior and learning ability. But not many know that medication can also properly make more alert a listless daydreamer by increasing his attention span and improving his ability to concentrate. Many, including those in the medical profession, think only in terms of prescribing medication for hyperkinesis while too few know that medication can also be used to improve significantly a short attention span, poor concentration, distractibility, handwriting and printing, visual perception and fidgetiness. They may or may not know that medication can also reduce tempers, mood swings, hostility and certain types of headaches, stomach aches, sleep problems and other ailments associated with learning disabilities.

For years the etiology of speech problems was thought to be psychological. Now a new inventory of special medication has proven helpful in cases of stuttering and cluttering, indicating that certain speech problems also can be neurologically caused in part or in whole.

The application of neurology to learning disabilities may startle some professionals. But research shows conclusively that a high percentage of learning problems are neurological in origin. However, the neurological aspect is only a part of the whole and must be considered along with all the other aspects of learning problems.

A high percentage of juvenile delinquents and drug addicts are poor readers, even though the same offenders have college-level IQs. This lends urgency to the fight to prevent learning disabilities and to rehabilitate those already trapped by this subtle despair.

The total approach must be used to provide individual help for each troubled student so that he may develop, learn, grow and eventually take his place as a well integrated whole person in our modern society.

LIST OF ILLUSTRATIONS

CONTENTS

CHAPTER ONE

THE ELUSIVE CURE

Two anxious parents leaned forward in their chairs one day in the principal's office of a suburban elementary school and listened hopefully as the school psychologist outlined a remedy for Billy, their third-grade boy. Half way through the principal interrupted.

"I'm sorry," he said, "but we've tried that already and it doesn't work in this case."

Little Billy was not learning in spite of a good IQ, a good school, an involved teacher, a concerned principal and dedicated but frustrated parents. The dilemma was regrettably familiar: "We've done this before; it's not the answer."

The principal suggested Billy's parents take him for a physical checkup, only to be told by the doctor their child was healthy and would probably "grow out of his problem."

The parents next arranged for private tutoring. They obtained the counsel of several other child psychologists recommended by the school who attempted to establish better understanding between child and parents. These sessions served to ease the tension that exists when children do not live up to parental expectation for learning and yet have the ability to do so.

And yet, despite all these efforts, Billy's attitude improved only slightly, thus aiding the behavioral aspect of the problem, but his learning disability remained unchanged.

Family after family hears the verdict: "The problem is that we've done this before, but it's not the answer. Something is missing." The acknowledgement of an unresolved problem is at least a step toward a solution.

The problem is not borne only by parents. Children who suffer learning disabilities inwardly yearn just as intensely and even more so for success. They are frequently misunderstood when they use unacceptable, and sometimes destructive, attention-getting devices. Such negative compensating adjustments are cries for help caused by frustrating problems of underachievement in education.

"Underachievement in Education" means being significantly behind (one or more years) in grade-level ability in reading, spelling, arithmetic or handwriting. It can be with or without an associated behavior problem. The younger the child, the less pronounced the degree of underachievement in learning.

The IQ Factor

A sizable number of students with educational problems today are in the mid-normal or low-dull normal IQ range. However, there are others with higher or lower IQs who also may be underachieving. Underachieving in education takes in the full range of IQs, starting with the lower IQ of the trainable mentally retarded (TMR), usually under 50, or the educable mentally retarded (EMR) whose IQ is usually under 75, right up the entire scale of normal IQs and into the genius category of 140 and over.

It must be emphasized that one's expected achievement level is determined by his IQ, and not by the chronological age and grade level. A high IQ does not automatically mean a student is immune from learning problems (Krippner 1968).

The logical method of spotting underachievement is by noting that a child is not learning properly in his normal grade level. On the other hand, children who may be earning proper grades for their grade level may still be underachieving in their elementary education because they have superior IQs. Sometimes this situation is spotted by behavior rather than by poor grades.

These behavioral problems can take the form of uncontrollable tempers . . . acting out . . . boredom . . . or destructive acts which sometimes lead to malicious mischief.

Mary was an unlikely candidate for the ranks of the tiny unfortunates. She was earning A's in the fifth grade. Her home situation was considered to be very normal. She was hyperactive, unlike a lot of her peers.

A psychological study revealed an IQ of 137. A neurological examination showed symptoms of hyperkinesis and some other neuro-perceptual signs, including an electroencephalogram (EEG) which revealed minimal abnormality.

Fifth-grade Mary should have been doing seventh- or eighth-grade work, therefore her satisfactory work limited to the fifth-grade level indicated she was definitely an underachiever. In her case, the high grades were misleading.

Behavior as a Clue

Ten-year-old Frank was well known in school, but not for good citizenship! He had become an increasingly difficult child with each succeeding year. Frank repeated first grade . . . barely scraped through second and third. Unless a miracle were to change him, the boy would not be ready academically to move with his class to the fifth grade the following fall.

The problem: Frank simply could not read.

An additional puzzling factor was Frank's normal IQ. Because of it, his parents, friends and educators assumed he was just not trying hard enough and didn't care.

Failure in proper diagnosis at this point caused a series of regrettable negatives in this young fellow's experience. Inability to read caused Frank to fall behind his peers at school. Consequently, Frank felt rejected by them. His lack of reading skill resulted in poor grades on report cards so his mother and father added to the feelings of rejection by scolding their son.

Since he could not achieve success by positive means Frank turned to negative ones to gain attention that he interpreted as "success." He became notorious as a "bad actor," so determined was he for recognition. This sort of behavior gave him a kind of "negative success." The pattern was drawn early for the troubled boy—all because he could not read.

Frank's parents by now recognized their son's obvious inability to master primer reading in first grade—even the second time around. So they engaged a private tutor for remedial reading assistance. This made little difference in Frank's progress (Krippner 1968). He simply could not learn to read.

The teachers and the tutor were not to blame for Frank's problem. It was more deep-seated than surface considerations could determine. The diagnosis required proper evaluation and testing to determine the type of reading problem suffered by the boy.

Reading is a complex function of the brain and certain of its appendages including the eye, ear and mouth. In addition the reader needs the coordination and balance of other functions of his nervous system in order to extract meaning from little symbols on a piece of paper. But Frank's eyes, ears and mouth all functioned normally. He had a good brain. Then, why the reading problem?

'Overactive' Only One Symptom

Billy is a fourth grader, average in height, weight and appetite. He's not a complainer or a troublemaker. He never gives his teachers trouble. In fact, he is exceptionally well behaved.

"I hardly know he's around," remarked his teacher when discussing her pupil with his mother after PTA. "He is not one to bother other children or misbehave in any way."

"I'm thankful for that," his anxious mother replied, "but why aren't his grades better? His reading and spelling are poor. He dreads having to read aloud in class because some of the kids make fun of him."

"Children can be cruel," the teacher acknowledged, "and we are doing everything possible to correct the situation."

Billy's mother had more on her mind. "Another thing that concerns me," she said, "is Billy's nail biting. I hadn't thought much about it until a relative visited our house and brought it to my attention."

"What other characteristics about Billy concern you?" the teacher asked. Little flickers of insight into her pupil's true condition were coming to light, indicating that Billy's problem was deeper than she had originally thought.

"Well, he is quiet but fidgety and has a very short attention span," replied the mother. "Also, I have wondered why he doesn't like the games other boys his age like."

"This might be due simply to poor coordination," the teacher reasoned. "He can't throw a ball very well. It won't go where he aims it. His movements are a bit stiff and awkward."

"It isn't that he doesn't *want* to, or that he hasn't tried. I guess he just doesn't have the capacity for coordinated physical activity. I wonder what his future will be," the distraught mother mused.

The underactive or hypoactive child is relatively unnoticed. This is an added complication for the youngster because the true nature of his problem frequently goes unrecognized. On the other hand, overactive class disrupters and those with annoying behavioral problems receive constant attention and surveillance. "The wheel that squeaks the loudest," goes the old proverb, "gets the grease first."

IQs Reach a Limit

A large number of children with learning disabilities suffer the consequences of overactivity. However, their problem in learning may not be uncovered until the pupil has been in school several years.

Ray and Sue (not related) were "A" students until the boy reached the fifth grade and the girl the sixth. Then their grades began dropping suddenly to "C's" and "D's." Parents and teachers could detect no cause for the dramatic drop in achievement. Their home life was steady, their social relationships normal, and all other areas of life were conducive to good study habits and healthy achievement patterns.

Both students were quite overactive but still had normal-to-bright IQ's ranging between 115 and 120. Thus, their IQs had compensated academically for their overactivity. In the early grades they did not have to pay attention as long or concentrate as hard to learn as did a child with a lower IQ.

But as the school work became increasingly more difficult and as they advanced from grade to grade, they both reached the point where their excellent IQ no longer compensated for their basic inadequacies.

Humans are complex beings. That's why each individual holds the possibility for a great variety of learning and behavior problems. It is impossible to outline each set of problems in each person. Nevertheless, the knowledge of basic principles which can be applied to any situation or any set of circumstances will be useful in helping children who would otherwise go through school and later life as frustrated underachievers.

When the Past Is Not Prologue

In years gone by, and even now in some cases, causes of underachievement in education and treatment for same were determined purely on a socio-psychological basis. Many parents have been told that their own emotional problems (whether or not they had any) were causing their child to fall behind in his learning.

In some cases the parents' own situation probably caused or aggravated problems in their offspring. But can this be really a major cause? *Yes,* on the part of students in an out-patient or in-patient psychological or psychiatric clinic. *No,* on the part of the regular school population.

Psychological/psychiatric treatment has been helpful to some, but in an alarming number of cases it has been totally ineffective. The failure leaves pupils frustrated and the parents upset. Small comfort it is after spending much time and money on counseling for themselves and their child to discover that the emotional dilemma is better understood and is improved but that the learning problem has improved little or not at all.

Parents, children and educators continue to be frustrated because in cases like these only a partial solution is reached. Parents who can't afford the recommended counseling remain doubly frustrated.

The cases of two boys in a large metropolitan area are typical:

Jim's parents are divorced. Psychological personality testing has revealed some of the negative emotional feelings that one would expect from a boy in this situation. Obviously, Jim's poor school work was a result of his inadequate social environment—no father.

George's parents live together. His social environment is good, and he is emotionally secure, yet George's school work is poor, like Jim's. Psychological testing showed that George lacks confidence . . . his inferior feelings about himself due to a lack of academic success. Just like Jim.

Each boy has ability as indicated by his IQ. Jim has the added complication of a divided home, yet both are underachievers.

Obviously, there must be other factors bearing on these problems—and there are!

Mental Illness and Learning Disability

Children suffering from learning disabilities are often teased by peers who consider them to be mentally retarded or mentally ill. The child often asks adults about this. The answer should always be a definite *no*.

Learning disability, mental illness and retardation are not synonymous. They're not even necessarily interrelated. Some parents of underachievers know this intuitively.

"My kid is not nuts!" they say. "And we don't think he's retarded." And they are correct, in most cases.

For years professionals have attributed learning problems to psychological or emotional problems. This is definitely the case with some. There are those children whose learning capacities are retarded, but in many cases neither condition applies.

Sometimes this erroneous idea prevails because when a learning disability is discovered the child and his parents are referred to the school psychologist. This action may cause parents to feel that their child's problem is purely psychological.

School districts sometimes try to minimize this problem by giving its services less threatening titles such as, "Pupil Personnel Service," or "Guidance and Research Department," instead of "School Psychological Services," or some other misunderstood label.

The drama of misunderstandings is quite real in the lives of parents whose children are mistakenly diagnosed. In my office one day a distraught mother related her sad story. All her friends, it seemed, as well as the staff of the public school were ready to blame her for her child's learning problem.

Her son was a human dynamo . . . never still. Wherever this pint-sized cyclone traveled he left a trail of debris that spun off his perpetual activity. There was little doubt, the educators told this mother, that her son's emotional problems reflected those of her own.

One of her friends counseled her that she didn't love her child enough, that he felt rejected. Another was convinced that she and her husband were incompetent parents and didn't discipline the child properly. Still another cautioned that the child had too much discipline. Already troubled by the problem itself, these accusations caused the mother to feel even more guilty and inadequate as a mother and as a person.

To top it off, the woman's pastor bluntly told his parishioner that her boy's problem was that she wasn't active enough in the church . . . didn't pray enough . . . wasn't spiritual enough. That was the final blow that left the woman shattered and completely confused.

Actually, she was a good mother. She had carried out everything that was proper and reasonable, despite all the confusing input to her mental computer. Imagine this mother's relief when the true cause of her child's problem was determined and when adequate treatment succeeded in calming the child.

The tested methods of other years are valid in many cases. They are not necessarily to be discarded for the thesis of this book. But it is important to add the new approach so that appropriate cases can receive proper treatment—an approach detailed in the following chapter.

BIBLIOGRAPHY FOR CHAPTER ONE

Krippner, Stanley, Etiological Factors in Reading Disability of the Academically Talented in Comparison to Pupils of Average and Slow-Learning Ability, *The Journal of Educational Research,* Vol. 61, No. 6, pp. 275-279, Feb. 1968.

CHAPTER TWO

GETTING THE WHOLE PICTURE

Human beings are complex in their growth, structure and function. Consequently, additional methods of diagnosis and treatment should be sought continually for unresolved problems.

Complex beings with complex problems require complex assistance. This is true both for normal growth and development and in the diagnosis and/or treatment of difficulties.

There are no *single cure-alls* for complex problems. All resources are required to provide complex assistance. The law of cause and effect applies: one effect from one cause may only need one remedy; but if an effect has an apparent cause and the remedy for which results in only partial correction, then additional causes should be sought so that additional remedies might be added, thus making remediation as complete as possible.

Seeing All Sides

A child or teenager who is physically healthy should not be automatically considered beyond medical-psychological testing. The young person may be free of disease, but not free of improper bodily functions.

At present, an evaluation of a student underachieving in education should draw on the following resources: (1) Educational, (2) Psychological, (3) Sociological, and (4) Neurological.

The added dimension is the *neurological* element in seeking remedies for learning and behavioral problems. The prognosis in many neurological cases, which are suffered by 15 to 27 per cent (Botel 1968, Dubnoff 1965, and Meier 1971) of the school population in the United States, is good because medication alone produces good results with respect to improved brain function for approximately 80 per cent of the troubled in the author's private practice and in a survey made by a local school district. Dr. Wender (1971) in his book *Minimal Brain Dysfunction in Children,* says that there is a 50 to 70 per cent chance of good response and five to 10 per cent chance of the symptoms becoming worse. And when other specialized help is applied, further effectiveness can be charted. The added assistance might be visual motor, auditory, or tactile perceptual training techniques for a child having difficulty in these types of neurological development.

Seeing the "whole child" and using all the resources suggested for diagnosis and treatment has made a big difference in providing help for children with learning disabilities. Many of them might otherwise have grown up frustrated, suffering increasing negative feelings, dropping out of school, and becoming delinquent, addicted to drugs or alcohol, going onto the welfare rolls, characterized as social misfits, ne'er-do-wells—in short, frustrated adult underachievers.

The early solution of a child's problem leads to the greater possibility of a fuller, more meaningful, happier life both for them and for all with whom they associate.

The Danger of Tunnel Vision

It is natural for a person specializing in a given field to approach a problem with "tunnel vision," that is to see a problem only from the viewpoint of his particular field. Specialization is vital, but we cannot rely on the tunnel vision of a single specialty to provide all the answers to a problem involving many facets. Each expert must function in relation to the part he fulfills in the whole.

Take a child with a reading problem to a psychologist and he will most probably find a psychological or emotional inadequacy contributing to the difficulty.

An educator would no doubt discover an educational lack.

A medical examination might reveal medical problems contributing to the learning difficulty. Additional examinations by other specialists could reveal still other contributing or aggravating factors.

Each of the suggested helps might be legitimate without being able to explain or remedy the total problem. However, when all the "tunnels" are brought into perspective they provide an over-all view of the problem, greatly increasing the possibility of proper diagnosis and correction.

The diagram on page 11 shows how the several parts of a person's constitution fit together to make the whole. Notice first a large circle in which there are three smaller circles—each overlapping the others. One circle represents the physical aspect of the human being . . . another the psychological . . . and the third circle the religious or spiritual aspect.

A human being is one person, but there are three basic aspects to his make-up or personality. Each has a body, a soul and a spirit.

The body is basically his world consciousness. The psychological is

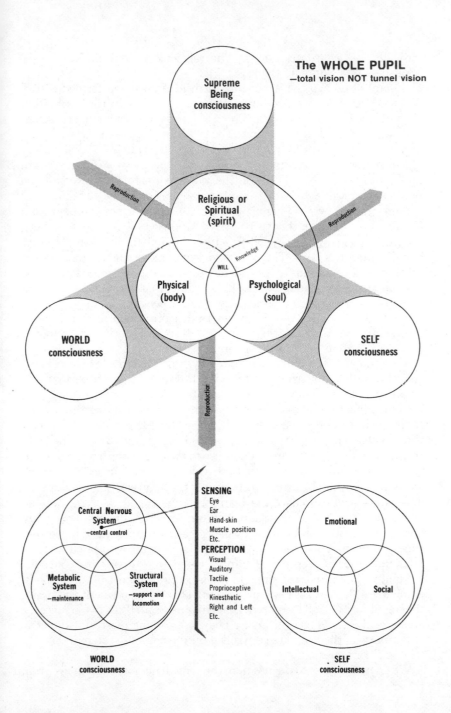

basically his self consciousness. The religious or spiritual is his consciousness of a Supreme Being.

Several years ago the American Medical Association formed a subdivision within its organizational framework to study the correlation between medicine and religion. The AMA thus was willing to give scientific, knowledgeable recognition to the fact that there is a Supreme Being and that man is incurably religious. He worships any of a wide variety of things from such inanimate objects as money and stones and trees to intangibles like a "Great Force" in the wide expanses of the universe. (The final chapter will deal with this phenomenon in greater detail.)

Note: In the overlapping aspects of the psychological and spiritual circles on the diagram there is the word "knowledge." It represents both a psychological and a spiritual function. Animals have a soul, but not a spirit. Man has both. The psychological circle in the diagram representing the soul expands to another circle which also accommodates three overlapping, interrelated circles. These smaller circles represent the intellectual, emotional and social aspects of a person.

In similar fashion, there is the expanded projection from the circle representing the physical (the body) into the central nervous system, the metabolic system and the structural system.

This chapter does not touch on every aspect of the "whole person" concept. Rather, it attempts to amplify those areas that are particularly meaningful to the twin accomplishments of learning and reading.

Concerning the metabolic system, we merely mention that the thyroid hormone has an effect on every cell in the body. It regulates each cell's use of fuel and nutrients to obtain heat and energy and to allow the body to function. This regulation extends also to the cells of the brain. So, when there are inappropriate amounts of thryoid hormone (particularly a lack of supply), the metabolism of the body and the brain can become sluggish. This slow-down can effect the learning process.

The structural system of the person concerns the support of the body and its locomotion. Mounting evidence seems to indicate that certain types of impaired body balance and coordination are associated with an inability to learn properly. (Chapter 15 enlarges upon this concept.)

Finally, the third or top circle in the large circle representing the body emphasizes the central nervous system. This is composed of the brain, the spinal cord and all the nerves that emanate from these two structures and spread throughout the entire body, controlling most of it directly. Other parts of the body are controlled by the nervous system indirectly through hormones.

We do not propose to discuss here the central nervous system in detail, but only to mention those organs and their commensurate function which specifically relate to learning and reading. These are listed to the right of the circle to show how they relate to the central nervous system.

The body has five basic senses. The sensing organs listed on the chart and related to the central nervous system are of particular interest to this study. These contribute to their respective perceptual functions in the brain.

For example, the eye picks up the image of an object and transmits it to the brain. There the actual perceptual function of vision takes place.

The ear picks up a sound but the perception of the vibrations is done by the auditory portion of the brain.

The hand or the skin touches something but the actual sensation of feeling is done by the tactile perception area of the brain.

Many people are unaware that their muscles, regardless of position, transmit the location of that position to the brain. This is called "proprioception"—another perceptual function required of the brain.

The perceiving of the directions of right and left involves also the perceptive function of the central nervous system.

The acts of sensing and perceiving are not just mechanical flesh and blood functions of the body. They are also integrated and interrelated with psychological functions.

Consider a child whose basic perceptual functions are inadequate or which function improperly, making him unable to perceive correctly the physical world in which he lives. If he cannot contact the physical world with adequate reality he probably will develop the types of emotional problems that result from the lack of adequate reality.

An approach to the problem from the psychological circle shows that the nervous system is affected by emotions, by intellectual ability and by social awareness. Every psychological function of the person is only realized through the medium or agency of the central nervous system. Emotional problems in the home or within the child can have an undesirable effect upon his learning ability. Inadequate social situations or excessive social pressures can also have an effect on learning. Emotional and social difficulties both can directly affect the proper physical functioning of the nervous system and consequently of the entire body.

It is therefore evident that many positive and negative factors can be involved in the complex process of learning. A person is but the sum of all his parts which function dependently upon each other in dramatic cohesion. The destiny of each human being is determined not by isolated factors but by the inter-working of his whole being. Tunnel vision must give way to total vision if adequate treatment is to be administered.

BIBLIOGRAPHY FOR CHAPTER TWO

Botel, Morton, Therapy and Therapeutic Advice: Methods and Systems for Teaching Dyslexic Pupils, *Dyslexia, Diagnosis and Treatment of Reading Disorders,* edited by **Keeney,** Arthur H., and **Keeney,** Virginia T., chapter 12, p. 121, the C.V. Mosby Company, St. Louis, 1968.

Dubnoff, Belle, Sequential Perceptual Motor Exercises, *Manual for Dubnoff School Program*—Level 1, Part 1, Teaching Resources, Subsidiary of The New York Times, 1965.

Meier, John H., Prevalence and Characteristics of Learning Disabilities Found in Second Grade Children, *Journal of Learning Disabilities,* Vol. 4, No. 1, pp. 10-11, January, 1971.

Wender, Paul H., *Minimal Brain Dysfunction in Children,* chapter 5, p. 127, Wiley-Interscience, a Division of John Wiley & Sons, Inc., New York, London, Sydney, Toronto, 1971.

CHAPTER THREE

FINDING THE PLAYS THAT WIN

One thing is forever good;
That one thing is Success.
Emerson—*Fate*

Resolved: *If proper treatment is to be applied, one must first recognize that a certain problem exists and then specifically identify the condition.*

The Plan for Recognition

A plan is effective only by those who know how to use it. In the treatment of a child with learning disabilities someone must be able to recognize his problem, be able to implement the specific diagnostic measures which serve as guides to proper treatment, and assess what degree of correction may be expected.

Correction requires team work. All members must be well informed. The team may include the parent, the teacher, the principal and his assistant, the special education supervisor and special teachers, the nurse, the school physician, the family physician, the school psychologist and his staff and possibly others.

People who fail to recognize a problem may do so for various reasons: (1) They may not be trained observers in that particular field, (2) They may have the same problem themselves, or (3) The problem may exist in their family and serve as an embarrassment. The observers who prefer *not* to see a problem in themselves or in their family may also fail to see it in someone else. Sometimes a person fails to diagnose the problem simply because he doesn't want to become involved.

Common questions follow, along with their answers.

1   *Is it possible to have discrepancies or disagreement between teachers, regarding the presence of a problem in a given child?*

Yes. Such a situation is quite possible and can be accounted for because of a difference in a child's ability in different types of classes. The problem

— JulieAune —

child may do well in mathematics, for example, but be poor in reading and spelling.

Another opportunity for disagreement lies in the attitudes of different teachers toward problem children or toward children with learning disabilities and the knowledge teachers have of the problem. Some pupils act and perform quite differently depending on whether the teacher is male or female. This variation of attitude is often learned at home in his response to mother and dad.

2 *Can different environmental situations affect and produce different behavior which in turn bear on a child's behavior and performance?*

Environment does have an enormous effect on a child's behavior and performance. Many pupils with learning disabilities perform better in smaller classes; many improve considerably when their instruction is on a one-to-one basis (one teacher to one child). But aside from private tutoring, this is practically impossible in public schools.

A child's behavior at home may be entirely different from his conduct at school. And in the doctor's office he can act in still another way. Sometimes a hyperactive pupil who can't sit still in school will sit calmly in a doctor's office with little or no manifestation of excessive activity. The physician, noting the child's exemplary behavior, is reluctant to prescribe medication for overactivity.

All the people guiding a problem child's life must first be urged to look at the youngster as a "whole person" and also to take a "whole situation" viewpoint. This involves a full view of the child's behavior and performance in all situations—particularly his learning at school.

3 *Can a basic rule be established in recognizing problems based on the social, economic, emotional and cultural backgrounds of these children with learning disabilities?*

Learning problems surface in all types of situations. Children from upper socio-economic situations are not automatically exempt. On the other hand, just because a pupil comes from a home that is culturally deprived and in which finances are low does not mean he automatically has a learning problem. However the greater the degree of instability in the emotional climate at home the greater the learning difficulty.

4 *When is the best time to recognize and treat learning problems?*

The earlier any problem is recognized and treatment begun the greater the chance of correction and the shorter the time required.

Schools should recognize a learning problem in kindergarten or in the first grade. Even more desirable is treatment in pre-school years.

Many things signal learning problems in pre-school children: overactivity, speech problems, delayed speech, inability to sit up alone, crawl, walk or ride a tricycle or bike at the age when most children do. Other symptoms include irritability, fussiness, temper tantrums, breath holding to the point of becoming blue then fainting, and the inability to take or to respond to discipline as other children do.

The benefits of early diagnosis by teachers are borne out in a review of the eighteen lowest achievers in remedial reading entering the seventh grade in one intermediate school. The principal copied from the Cumulative School Record of each student the comments made by the teacher indicating academic difficulty and the grade in which it was recorded. Eleven of the eighteen notations were made by kindergarten teachers . . . five by first-grade teachers . . . and two by second-grade teachers.

The comments varied. Some were: "very immature," "reading is difficult," "slow learner," "little or no desire for school work," "short attention span," "very shy and quiet," "can't sit still and concentrate," "shows little interest," "very slow worker," "slow in grasping concepts," and so on. A host of frustrations were wrapped up in each brief comment.

5 *What are typical manifestations of children with learning difficulties with or without behavioral problems?*

Such a child could have any one or a combination of seven basic manifestations. They are:

A *Hyperkinetic behavior or overactivity.*

This characteristic keeps the problem child always on the move. He runs instead of walks; he moves about instead of staying in his seat; he is fidgety instead of calm. Many of them are called "wall climbers" by their teachers. When their teachers do succeed in getting them to sit, the pupils have short attention spans and poor concentration. They are easily distracted. If they can be encouraged to start an assignment they rarely follow through and hardly ever finish an assignment.

B *Hypokinetic behavior or gross underactivity.*

This type of child sits like a bump on a log. He is a daydreamer without much energy even for things he likes to do. Lethargic and calm, he is described by teachers often as "simply no problem at all." However, close examination reveals usually that he too has a short attention span, poor concentration, is easily distracted and manifests a certain amount of fidgetiness and nervousness even though he remains in his seat.

Outwardly underactive, these children are actually suffering from a subtle hyperactivity as far as their nervous system is concerned.

C *Short attention span.*

Attention is short whether the child is listening to instructions or carrying them out once they have been understood. He finds it difficult to work long on a project or assignment. His mind wanders quickly from one item to another.

D *Labile emotions.*

Sudden changes in emotion characterize this child. His malady is often characterized by "mood swings." An emotionally labile child can be gay and happy one moment and sad or depressed the next. Now he is well behaved, the next moment he is fighting, throwing a temper tantrum or behaving in an inappropriate manner. Sometimes the bad behavior comes without any obvious provocation, just as do the sudden changes in emotion.

E *Performance fluctuations.*

Moment by moment, hour by hour, day by day or perhaps page by page the work of this type fluctuates. One moment the pupil may be doing acceptable work, the next accomplishing hardly anything at all. This child is frustrating not only to his teacher but also to himself. The teacher naturally admonishes him, believing his poor work shows lack of effort or desire. She knows he can do better. So does the child, but he is in the grip of his problem and it's hanging on hard.

The teacher's scolding or evident disappointment upsets this child further. He is trying to do his best and he does not understand why his work pattern fluctuates.

F *Perceptual disorders.*

These malfunctions can involve visual, auditory or tactile (touch) perception as well as other types of perception. They can include everything that is actually a neurological function of the brain—the perception of information being sent by the sense organ (eye, ear, or whatever is used for touching, etc.). When the mental image for some children is reversed, they see a word backwards or write a letter, word or number backwards.

Others have a visual motor perceptual problem which affects the manner in which they print, draw or write. A letter, instead of being switched side for side, will be switched top for bottom. An "M" can become a "W" or a "W" an "M". Letters are sometimes rotated only ninety degrees. An "n" becomes a "c."

G *Anti-social reactions.*

Children so inclined often become loners and isolates. They find it difficult to make friends either because of their tendency to withdraw or because of their frequent fights or difficulties with other pupils.

This type often develops disrespect for authority and becomes disobedient to his teacher, principal, and even his parents.

An extensive list of symptoms and specific behavior patterns manifested by children with learning disabilities is found in the book *Educationally Handicapped, a Handbook for Teachers* (Dr. Alice C. Thompson, 1966). Another excellent list is found in the monograph *Minimal Brain Dysfunction in Children* (Clements, 1966).

The Plan for Referral

Resolved: *Team work is essential in the treatment of children with learning problems. It is difficult to help a pupil singlehandedly.*

Anyone recognizing a learning problem in a child should report the observation immediately so that necessary studies can be performed. Immense satisfaction comes to the person who is first to recognize a learning problem. He becomes the key person of a team enlisted to help eliminate the problem.

There can be two types of referral: Referral to certain members of the team is essential, but to others referral is made only when their specialized help is needed. For example, a complete eye examination is necessary only for pupils with eye problems, etc. (See chapter six.)

A *A Preliminary Referral*

This initial referral by the teacher and principal of a pupil not learning adequately is for the purpose of ascertaining the child's basic ability and possible areas of handicap. The results of IQ achievement and perceptual testing provide the principal and teacher some specifics with which they can work in the regular classroom setup of the child's own school. It is of utmost importance to use every legitimate means to help a child in his regular school setting. Only when these alternate methods have been tried and shown to be ineffective in solving the learning problems should the pupil be referred for special class placement.

Alternate suggestions:

1 The school psychologist conferring with the principal can help determine whether the child would be better off with a well structured, a moderately structured or a loosely structured teacher. Teachers have different teaching styles. Some lecture exclusively, or lecture with audio-visual aids and so on. Pupils have different learning styles. Some learn visually, some are audio learners. In the area of response, some can perform

orally but cannot do written work. Teacher-pupil styles should be matched. Recommendations as to the sex, age and personality type of the teacher best suited for the child should be made by the school psychologist.

2   Remedial classes for the area(s) of weakness should be implemented where the teacher-student ratio is quite small. This teacher should know perceptual training techniques and also have the necessary equipment for the same.

3   Teacher aides and assistants in the regular or remedial classes should be enlisted to work with these pupils but under the direct guidance of the teacher.

4   A shortened-day contract with a flexible schedule should be available. For any given day the child can remain at school as long as he can participate in the program. When his behavior becomes unmanageable the teacher calls the parent who picks him up. The teacher must guard against being manipulated by the child. Some days will be shortened to as little as half an hour; other days he may last half the day; and some days he will not be sent home at all. Such a system needs to be explained thoroughly to the parents so they understand what is being done and why.

5   Medication has enabled many pupils to stay in regular classes who otherwise would have been assigned to a special education program.

6   Conferences involving any combination of parent-teacher-pupil-principal-school psychologist should be held in order for each person respectively to understand the home and school situations and thus be better able to help the child.

B   A Special Education Referral

When all attempts to help in the regular classroom prove ineffective, then the child should be referred for further study and be considered for special class placement.

Through a diagnostic workup, team members will provide the most complete picture of the problem, according to their specific fields. On the basis of this collected information the best program of correction available can be initiated on behalf of the youngster.

TEAM MEMBER	DIAGNOSTIC TASK
TEACHER	List the suggestive symptoms of the pupil (see the seven basic manifestations in this chapter). Outline briefly any other aspects of the problem.
SCHOOL NURSE	Eye vision tests (see chapter six) Snellen Telebinocular, Titmus or similar test is much preferred over Snellen test. Ear Test (see chapter six) Audiometer.
FAMILY PHYSICIAN	Information as to whether or not student is basically healthy. If not, what his health problems are, briefly.
SCHOOL PSYCHOLOGIST	Intelligence Quotient (IQ) tests Achievement tests in reading, spelling and arithmetic Personality tests Perceptual tests —is special remedial help needed? Evaluation of home emotional climate —recommend counseling as needed.
MEDICAL SPECIALIST **Eye doctor as needed**	Complete eye examination —are glasses needed? —are eye exercises needed? —are other corrective procedures needed?
Ear doctor as needed	Complete ear examination —are corrective measures needed?
Pediatrician or Neurologist or Learning & Behavior Specialist or Knowledgeable General Practitioner	Neurological examination designed for learning problems. —is medication needed? —any special recommendations regarding Physical Education participation, school restrictions regarding exercise, qualification for special class on a medical neurological basis?
SPEECH THERAPIST **as needed**	Identify speech problem —is speech therapy needed?
SPECIAL EDUCATION DIRECTOR	Aid in determining special educational needs.
REMEDIAL READING SPECIALIST —in the school —outside the school	Specify as much as possible, the reading disabilities present.
PHYSICAL EDUCATION SPECIALIST —for Coordinative Perceptual Exercises	Identify any area of inadequate or underdeveloped muscular function which is adding to the learning problem or causing improper development of an adequate self-image.

The completed diagnostic tasks furnish a total view of the subject's problem. Few "total views" are alike in every detail, because of the complex process of learning.

Modern techniques in observation, experimentation and research are constantly improving learning processes. What becomes a "total view" today may soon be only a partial view. Truly nothing is ever total or final in a man's lifetime. There is always more to learn and discover. Only God is complete. But the challenge to learn and discover is one of man's great delights and pleasures.

The Flow Chart on page 25 may be helpful in outlining possible team interaction and in suggesting a sequence for referral (Clements, 1966).

6   What diagnoses are used for these learning problems?

The names used for formal diagnoses are both general and specific. The following list is not intended to be complete. Experts use different terms for the same problems. This is more apt to occur in the use of the general terms rather than in the use of specific ones.

The problem of nomenclature exists in virtually every field of study. Standardization of names and terms is needed and would be helpful—particularly in new areas of learning such as these. The successful team member must be aware of the possible differences in terms of diagnostic procedures.

Some items are intentionally omitted from the lists.The term "epilepsy" is not included because the malady does not specifically involve a learning problem.

By the same token, a person with a learning problem because of neurological malfunctioning who has an abnormal EEG (brain wave test) is not automatically termed epileptic. The problem of epilepsy, or convulsive seizures, is a clinical diagnosis based on the type or nature of the seizure or convulsion exhibited by the patient. Unfortunately, the term "epilepsy" has a degree of social stigma attached to it. This is because of misinformation, a lack of information, or a lack of understanding of the correct information. The national and local societies for epilepsy have done much to set the record straight on behalf of those with epilepsy. The national office* is eager to provide material to interested citizens.

Some specialists prefer the terms "convulsive problem," or "seizure problem" instead of "epilepsy." These euphemisms protect the feelings and ego of these patients. (See chapter eight.)

---

*Epilepsy Foundation of America · 733 15th Street, N.W., Washington, D.C. 20005

Two other terms not found in the lists are "brain damage" and "brain injury." The vast majority of children with learning problems are physically and mentally healthy. They look great! Tarnopol (1971) makes a similar point. But put yourself in the position of a child who has been tagged as one suffering brain damage and you'll have some idea of the struggle inside as he questions what and who he really is. Such empathy will also help you identify with his parents. If you can truly experience their feelings you won't object to changing the terms to read "brain dysfunction," or "neurological impairment." These have a much less negative effect on the feelings and ego of both child and parent.

Children labeled wrongly have a difficult time developing an adequate self-image of acceptance and worth. They often lack self-competence. They are all too aware that their learning problem causes them to be different from their peers. The diagnosis of "brain damage" or "brain injury" just adds to their emotional trauma.

To compound the problem, unthinking adults often remind the child of his disability when he does not perform as they think he should. So just at a time when positive reassurance is desperately needed, a negative connotation of worth is implied.

DIAGNOSES

GENERAL

Hyperkinetic Syndrome
Minimal Brain Dysfunction
Neurological Impairment
Cerebral Dysrhythmia
Cerebral Dysfunction
Minimal Cerebral Dysfunction
Dyslexia

SPECIFIC

Visual perceptual problems
Visual discrimination problems
Auditory perceptual problems
Auditory discrimination problems
Tactile perceptual problems
Tactile discrimination problems
Visual motor perceptual problems
Dysgraphia
Strephosymbolia
Dyssymbolia
Chronic recurrent headaches associated with reading or learning
Hyperkinesis
Right and left confusion or reversal (directionality)
Poor self-concept
Personality problem
Character disorder
Anti-social behavior

There are other diagnoses which could be added, but these cover most of them. Some of the Specific Diagnoses can be further divided into even more detailed items such as the five basic types of visual perceptual problems.

The Plan for Treatment

Resolved: *A thorough diagnostic workup produces an accurate, detailed diagnosis. Therefore a more accurate and detailed diagnosis results in more specific and effective treatment.*

Since this is true, what should be the goal in treating young people with learning disabilities?

Obviously, the immediate goal is to improve learning and behavior to whatever degree possible. Whatever a person cannot correct he can adjust to with assistance from those who understand his problem. But should this be the total aim? Today's culture places heavy stress upon academic achievement, however this should not be the sum total of life's most important accomplishment. Emotional growth, self acceptance and social acceptance are also important. So are manual skills and other non-academic abilities.

History has honored the lives of great people who could neither read nor write but who were notable kings, rulers and artists. (Lloyd Thompson, 1971). The inability to read, write, spell or understand mathematics does not necessarily equal failure. On the other hand, these skills greatly increase a person's ability to be more successful in a wide range of endeavors in life.

The proper goal in treating learning disabilities should be:

1 To correct or reduce to a minimum any defects in the learning process.

2 To aid the pupil in achieving positive success experiences at whatever level and in whatever skill he functions best, simultaneously improving his self-image as well as his ability to learn.

3 To aid the pupil whose learning level remains low in gaining self-competence through other means such as counseling or in coordinative development exercise programs or in both.

Interested parties seeking treatment for learning disabilities have four basic community resources:

1 Medical

Medication *(see chapters eleven, sixteen and seventeen)*
Eye care *(see chapter six)*

WHO can do WHAT

Initial and subsequent steps when you suspect a Learning Problem.

Locate yourself along the left hand side of the page and see to whom the arrows direct you. The order of suggested preference to whom you should first contact or refer to next is from left to right. Professional contacts are made only with proper legal consent.

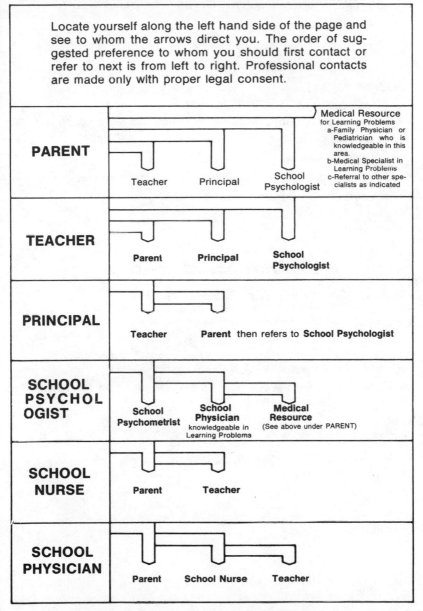

PARENT

Teacher — Principal — School Psychologist

Medical Resource
for Learning Problems
a-Family Physician or Pediatrician who is knowledgeable in this area.
b-Medical Specialist in Learning Problems
c-Referral to other specialists as indicated

TEACHER

Parent — Principal — School Psychologist

PRINCIPAL

Teacher — Parent then refers to School Psychologist

SCHOOL PSYCHOLOGIST

School Psychometrist — School Physician knowledgeable in Learning Problems — Medical Resource (See above under PARENT)

SCHOOL NURSE

Parent — Teacher

SCHOOL PHYSICIAN

Parent — School Nurse — Teacher

Ear care *(see chapter six)*

Hormonal, allergies, nutritional care *(see chapter seventeen)*

2 Special education

In the school *(see chapter twelve)*

Outside the school *(see chapter twelve)*

3 Counseling

For the pupil *(see chapter fourteen)*

For the parent (in or outside the school) *(see chapter thirteen)*

For both *(see chapter fourteen)*

4 Physical education

Coordination development and perceptual-motor training *(see chapter fifteen)*

BIBLIOGRAPHY FOR CHAPTER THREE

Clements, Sam D., *Minimal Brain Dysfunction in Children, NINDB* Monograph No. 3, Phase 1, Public Health Service Publication No. 1415, Section 6, pp. 11-13, U.S. Department of Health, Education and Welfare, Washington, D. C., 1966.

Tarnopol, Lester, *Learning Disorders in Children, Diagnosis, Medication, Education,* chapter 1, pg. 4, Little, Brown and Co., Boston, 1971.

Thompson, Alice C., *Educationally Handicapped, a Handbook for Teachers,* California State College at Los Angeles, 1966.

Thompson, Lloyd J., Language Disabilities in Men of Eminence, *Journal of Learning Disabilities,* Vol. 4, No. 1, pp. 39-45, January, 1971.

CHAPTER FOUR

THE MANY CAUSES OF LEARNING PROBLEMS

Basic Principle: "Complex beings with complex problems require complex assistance, whether for normal growth and development or in the diagnosis and correction of abnormalities."

Basic Principle: "Complex problems often have multiple causes."

Basic Principle: "When a problem persists after a single cause has been treated, additional causes must be uncovered."

Fledgling-physicians are taught in medical school not to overlook the possibility of a second diagnosis or even more in treating disease. The same rule applies in the complicated process of treating learning disabilities and associated behavior problems.

Doctors once thought that the primary cause of learning problems was simply physical trauma, but this is no longer believed. Studies have shown that the primary cause in the high percentage of cases is hereditary. (Goldberg 1968, Chalfant & Scheffelin 1969, Rossi, 1970). Specific difficulties are passed on to children through the genetic process by means of the chromosomes and genes by someone else in the family tree who had a similar problem. Patterns of these genetic problems are seen in some families. (Silver 1971.) Physical trauma can still cause learning problems and emotional difficulties. (Towbin 1971.) "Physical trauma" includes such things as difficulties a mother might have during her pregnancy, labor or delivery. Or it might refer to difficulties a child might have in the neo-natal period just after birth and the few weeks following. It can also refer to head injury resulting from a blow or caused by a fall. All the causes of physical trauma are not known.

There are also the diseases of the nervous system, such as an infection in the brain tissue itself whether caused by bacteria or by a virus.

Then there are diseases such as the measles (Rubeola) which, on rare occasion, can have a brain or cerebral complication causing serious inflammation of the brain tissue, called measles encephalitis.

Poor nutrition can also bring about physical harm to the brain and nervous system. High fever from any cause can also produce physical deterioration in the brain.

A recent study done at Harbor General Hospital in Torrance, California, by Kenneth Zike, M.D., involving 300 patients, showed that the primary cause of learning problems was neurological in 75 per cent, emotional in 15 per cent and 10 per cent were indeterminable. These patients had been referred to the EH (Educationally Handicapped) Clinic by their school district.

The study of causes in this area must acknowledge the emotional factor in children with learning problems who are either in a mental hospital or in a psychiatric outpatient facility. Physical trauma or disease would certainly be a high factor in a hospital or outpatient clinic dealing with those children who have a learning problem but who also have obvious physical difficulty such as those with Cerebral Palsy. On the other hand, a study conducted by a regular school where the vast majority of children are obviously healthy in body and sound in mind with normal emotional development, would show that physical causes are minimal and that either the mother or father or both or some other near relative also had and probably still has a learning problem.

The diagram on the opposite page deals with the Functions, Factors and Facilities affecting learning and behavior. The chart graphically portrays functions of mankind on a physical, psychological and spiritual basis. It shows the chief factors influencing mankind, which are the main thrust of this chapter. It deals with the hereditary, the spiritual and moral, the psychological, the physical, and the unknown causes. The chart also deals thirdly with the facilities for mankind that are available for assisting and helping with learning, as well as other problems.

When parents learn that heredity plays a part in the cause of learning disability, they are often relieved because the finding indicates that they did not do something or omit something that led to their child's problem. This observation is extremely important. When parents are relieved of guilt and anxiety and from personal blame, negative feelings vanish. They can act positively in correcting the problem.

Psychiatric and psychological resources today tend to place much of the blame for learning problems squarely on the parents. Of course there is enormous influence generated by parents upon their children. But undue emphasis on this assertion does more harm than good. Remember, there are usually multiple causes that lead to learning problems. Recognition and treatment of the problem are more important by far than seeking out the cause(s).

People who are quick to blame parents must be reminded that they

Functions, Factors and Facilities Affecting Learning and Behavior

Complex Beings with Complex Problems Require Complex Assistance whether for:

Normal Growth and Development or

Diagnosis and Correction of Abnormalities.

Such assistance involves **the cooperative effort of all resources.** Singular or unilateral measures are often ineffective in complex issues.

FUNCTIONS OF MANKIND

Physical
See
Hear
Touch
Taste
Smell
Move on land, sea, air and space
Grow
Sustain
Reproduce
Love
Etc.

Psychological
Think
Know more and more
Act (choose)
Develop skills and habits
Respond emotionally
Socialize
Invent, discover, produce
Communicate (speech, writing, attitude)
Decide
Judge
Perceive
Control
Submit
Love
Develop and maintain a proper self-concept

Spiritual
Worship
Pray
Praise
Am thankful
Love
Etc.

FACTORS INFLUENCING MANKIND

Hereditary
Genetic
Mimicry

Spiritual and Moral
Home
Religious training
Educational
Social
Intrinsic sinful nature
Demonic

Psychological
Home
Educational
Social
Prenatal and Neo-natal

Physical
Home
Social
Medical-preventive-curative
Nutritional
Brain injury
Metabolic
Infectious
High fever
Prenatal
Natal and Neo-natal
Instincts
Allergic
Unknown

FACILITIES FOR MANKIND

Family
Educational
Medical
Social
Religious
Mental
Civic
Legal
Political   Etc.

would have also to blame the parents of the parents for the problem, going all the way up the family tree to Adam and Eve.

A psychologist friend of mine once reminded a group of us that any who would point the finger of judgment at Adam and Eve should be careful because in doing so they admit that anyone else—including the one who judges—might err just as badly!

Before a specialist can designate a certain physical condition, disease or event as the cause of a learning problem he must first observe distinct changes in the child's performance educationally, emotionally and psychologically before and after the physical event occurred. For example, a child may suffer a severe blow on the head and become unconscious. He might be hospitalized with the diagnosis of brain concussion. Yet that child may recover without any specific measurable differences in his ability to learn and behave properly following the incident.

On the other hand, another child may suffer the same type of injury and recover with different effects on his behavior and learning or on both. But even in this situation the specialist must consider multiple causes. That second child might have inherited a learning problem that didn't surface until the injury took place. The accident might actually lead indirectly to a serious learning disability.

The same observation could be made concerning an emotional upset which also could produce a learning problem. It might be one factor in a series that led to complications. All this emphasizes the complexity of the entire problem.

One of the purposes for establishing the causes is to bring reassurance to parents . . . to remove the false guilt that plagues them. The truth that many learning problems are hereditary helps relieve those parents by minimizing their negative ego feelings so they can become positively involved in the program of treatment.

Other parents may react despondently if the cause produces or reinforces guilt feelings. Some might feel that if it is hereditary, nothing can be done, but help is available for learning problems regardless of cause.

BIBLIOGRAPHY FOR CHAPTER FOUR

Chalfant, J.C., and **Scheffelin,** M.A., Central Processing Dysfunctions in Children: A Review of Research, *NINDS* Monograph No. 9, chapter 8, Section on Genetic Factors, pp. 97-98, U.S. Department of Health, Education, and Welfare, Bethesda, Md., 1969.

Goldberg, H.K., *Dyslexia,* chapter 10, p. 90, **Keeney** and **Keeney,** editors, the C.V. Mosby Co., St. Louis, 1968.

Rossi, Albert O., Genetics of Higher Level Disorders, *Journal of Learning Disabilities,* Vol. 3, No. 8, pp. 387-390, August, 1970.

Silver, Larry B., Familial Patterns in Children with Neurologically-Based Learning Disabilities, *Journal of Learning Disabilities,* Vol. 4, No. 7, pp. 349-358, Aug-Sept., 1971.

Towbin, Abraham, Organic Causes of Minimal Brain Dysfunction: Perinatal origin of Minimal Cerebral Lesions, *Journal of the American Medical Association,* Vol. 217, No. 9, pp. 1207-1214, Aug. 30, 1971.

CHAPTER FIVE

HOW READEST THOU?

The act of reading and the ability to comprehend the text are complex procedures most of us take for granted. Those who find it easy assume that it's easy for all, but it's not.

"What do you mean you can't read?" they demand of the less fortunate. "You just haven't tried! Anyone can read if he wants to!"

Unfortunately, that's not true. Our learning, in large measure, is based upon our reading. Good readers are usually good learners. The opposite is also true.

Reading isn't simply looking at letters . . . words . . . sentences . . . paragraphs and then translating them into thought. The process of reading is a highly complex function integrating many facets of a human being who is the only creature on earth with such wondrous capability. Reading is indispensable in this modern, civilized world. It is necessary in the quest of an education, of good employment and of satisfying recreation. A high percentage of the information provided for formal education is on the printed page. Much of the information we use in daily life at home, at work and at play appears in printed form.

I feel certain that in the future, information will be supplied increasingly on tape and via audio transmission techniques. People unable to read adequately will thereby improve their station by those media. But for the present, we must concentrate our thinking on training children to use existing media and they require the ability to read and to read rapidly with comprehension.

One aspect of the reading process which we still need to research further is the physical function of the eyes as they pick up the image being scanned. These images are transmitted to the seeing area of the brain and sent to other parts of the brain where these images can be associated with other senses, thus giving fuller meaning to what is being observed. Placing meaning upon words is not only an intellectual function of the mind. It is also an emotional or psychological function of the mind.

Those who enjoy a stable, adequate emotional climate find it much easier to attach intellectual meaning as well as emotional feeling to words observed. For example, some children (and adults too) can accurately grasp the sound or phonics and properly handle intonation and grammar but can't get beyond this mechanical process. They can't attach meaning to what they've read. Some have trouble only with certain words, others with sentences and eventually whole paragraphs.

Some can't comprehend what they're reading unless they mouth the words being read. Others must speak the words loudly enough for their ears to hear and thus reinforce the reading mechanism by adding the auditory to the visual. The moving of the tongue, mouth and throat muscles silently adds the tactile (touch) and proprioceptive (muscle position sense) senses to the visual and thus reading is accomplished.

Chapter six will deal more specifically with the full function of reading, and chapter seven will be devoted to the function of the brain.

The need for reading and learning on the part of someone with learning disability is stressed because of its prime importance in our society. But there are other functions which need attention also, such as spelling and arithmetic, etc. These are also important. But a concentration on reading will keep the issue uncomplicated at this point. However, the same approach to reading difficulties can also be used in treating other problems with learning.

Each aspect of the reading problem must be evaluated to determine what problems exist to prevent a pupil from reading adequately. These aspects include the physical, the perceptual, the neurological, the emotional, the electro-chemical, the hormonal and other phenomena. A broader description of each is considered separately in chapters to follow.

Several pages of outline are given to this subject in the article, "Bases of Classification of Reading Disorders" (Blom & Jones 1970). It gives those interested a fuller and more concise outline of all that is involved in reading.

Rare is the child in our world who does not wish to read well . . . who is not mustering every force to achieve this important skill for daily living. There are vast numbers of adults too who wish their reading abilities could be improved. Both are frustrated by their underachievement. We can be thankful that children today have available to them helps of many types designed to assist them in overcoming their handicaps.

A reading problem, like any other problem, should be attacked scientifically by use of the law of cause and effect. A problem usually has a cause or several causes which can be found. When this is accomplished through research and investigation the door is open to remediation. If you, or someone you know, has a reading problem, do your utmost immediately to find help to overcome this frustrating handicap.

The word "cause" in the paragraph above refers to the specific mis-function of the central nervous system that produces the learning prob-lem. It might be poor visual perception or inadequate auditory discrim-ination and not the "cause" referring to heredity or to delayed breathing at birth, or to brain concussion, or to a number of suspected gremlins which might be nothing more than scapegoats.

"Reading maketh a full man," wrote Sir Francis Bacon many years ago. The adage is more true today than ever.

BIBLIOGRAPHY FOR CHAPTER FIVE

Blom, Gaston E. and **Jones,** Arlene W., Bases of Classification of Reading Disorders, *Journal of Learning Disabilities,* Vol. 3, No. 12, pp. 606-617, December, 1970.

THE EYE AND THE EAR

Do we really see with our eyes?

Not altogether. Actually, the eye is merely our "television camera" that picks up an image and projects it on the inside back portion of the eye, the retina. There it is actually upside down because the eyeball has only a simple lens system.

This image on the retina stimulates millions of little components of our nervous system which in turn transmit the image along the nerve of the eye (optic nerve) back to the rear of the brain (the occipital area) where the image is actually "seen" or perceived. The perceived image can be likened to a TV screen, although it is not actually a "screen."

The actual process by which we see something is still a great mystery. When the information collected by the eye arrives in the back part of the brains of most of us the occipital area correctly perceives the image. But the images in some occipital areas are incorrectly perceived. Some may be reversed (a "b" would become a "d" or "saw" would become "was"); some may be inverted top for bottom (an "m" would become a "w" or vice versa). Right and left aspects of objects are a learned item. Some learn it more quickly than others and some never learn it at all. There are adults who still do not know their right from their left.

Whenever the seeing part of the brain perceives a visual mental image it sends it to the visual memory bank and also to different associational areas. Take the matter of reading, for example. You look at a word . . . the eye picks it up and transmits it to the brain which perceives it in the area described. Now a meaning must be assigned to that word.

The teacher pronounces the word and gives the meaning. The part of the brain which hears (the temporal area) must learn what particular sound goes along with the letters and syllables that make up the word. Then that part of the brain has to tell the part of the brain concerned with speech how the muscles of the throat and chest and neck and mouth region should form the appropriate sounds. Obviously this is an inter-related function with hearing.

In the same way that eyes serve as cameras, our ears are microphones that pick up sound and transmit it to the brain along the hearing nerve track (the acoustic nerve). The sound reaches the ear through the medium of air; the vibrations are picked up by the outside visible ear and funneled down the ear canal to the ear drum which translates the sound into mechanical vibrations along the three tiny bones in the middle ear. Through them the sound reaches the last bone, the base of which is a bony diaphragm which transfers these vibrations to the inner ear liquid.

These three little bones never change in size. They are just as large in a newborn baby as in a seventy-year-old adult. The liquid transmits the vibrations to nerve endings which translate the information into electrical-chemical signals. These are sent along the hearing or "acoustic" nerve to the hearing part of the brain in the temporal lobe where the sound is perceived. Therefore we do not "see" with our eyes or "hear" with our ears. It is all done by the brain.

The brain could not see or hear without the eye and ear, of course. The eye picks up the sight for the brain to see and the ear collects the sound for the brain to hear. Again, this neurophysiological function, or electrical-chemical function, is not completely understood.

Just as vision has memory areas, so does sound. The brain has associational areas for sound and sight. It's not just eyes and ears. They are sensory organs that pick up information and send it to the brain—the master computer center—which perceives the messages. Each time the brain perceives something it attaches a concept to what is being seen or heard or touched or smelled or tasted. The amount of function and interrelationship, and the variety and complexity of all this is beyond human imagination.

This brief allusion is offered merely to illustrate how the least interruption can cause these delicately balanced organs to malfunction. If a child does not see a given letter the same way consistently, how can he put a consistent sound to it or attach a consistent meaning? And if the child cannot put a consistent concept with a word perceived how can he have a consistent and uniform understanding of its meaning? If his understanding is not consistent how can he use the symbol properly to achieve practical use of the word or item observed?

The same process is involved in writing. You cannot wield a pencil unless the eye is seeing properly or unless the eye memory bank can recall items from the past. The vision portion of the brain sends information to the motor portion of the brain which controls hand muscle function. Then the muscles are told how to move properly. As the pencil of the writer begins to move the eye double-checks on what the fingers are writing. This emphasizes a basic principle: one cannot write anything that he is not seeing at the moment or that he cannot perceive from past visual memory. One cannot speak any word or meaningful sound which his ear hasn't heard in the past and stored in his hearing or auditory memory area. Any distortion at the receiving end or at the perceiving end leads to faulty incoming or outgoing communication. Input and output are linked and any point along the route of this complex mechanism can be upset and can produce difficulty and improper functions.

More information on the brain will be presented in the following chapter concerning the function of this amazing organ.

Eye Examination

The most important eye testing done in the school is the test for visual acuity of the eyeball using the Snellen Chart. Other devices such as the Telebinocular or Titmus apparatus test for muscle balance as well as for visual acuity. These tests, which may be done by the school, tell only how the eyes perform optically. Many people have excellent visual acuity who suffer impaired visual perception. Those with visual acuity problems should follow the guidelines below as they seek assistance in overcoming the problem. These guidelines were drawn up at a meeting with two ophthalmologists from Whittier, California. They are designed to aid school nurses in the testing and disposition of children in whom a possible eye problem exists:

1   The ideal time to have a child's eyes examined thoroughly and routinely by a specialist (if there have been no other obvious eye or vision problems) is at the pre-school age of four years. Testing is always indicated any time there is an abnormal condition of the eyes or vision.

2   The Snellen Chart is a means of detecting eye problems. Plus lenses are used to determine farsightedness (hyperopia) which may at times cause a reading problem. Anyone can administer the test, but only a specialist can interpret it to determine if any corrective measures are needed. Each eye should be checked separately, and afterward the two together.

3   Referral for an eye examination should be made and *a referral note should be sent to the doctor.*

a.   When any school child has symptoms of eye strain from reading, such as headache, red eyes, eye-ache, tired eyes, blurred vision, watery eyes or a frequent headache problem at the end of the school day, or a dislike of reading, or odd positions of the head while reading. The teacher or nurse should ask the pupil such questions as, "When you read, does the printing become blurry in 10 to 15 minutes?"

b.   When a child is in a special reading class or is one grade level below in reading achievement.

c.   When a kindergartener has 20/40 vision in both eyes or worse, or the vision of one eye being one line or more different on the Snellen Chart from the other eye. (Example: Right eye 20/40, Left eye 20/30.) *Confirm the Snellen findings by redoing the test one week later.* Refer *only* when findings persist.

d.   When a pupil in first grade or above has 20/30 vision or a one-line difference or more on the Snellen findings. Repeat the test one week later. Refer only if the findings persist.

e.   When a child cannot converge (cross) his eyes at a point 120 mm. or 4¾ inches in front of them and also has the symptoms described in 3a above.

f.   When a child whose eyes do not look together or which do not track together, or if one eye from time to time drifts by itself (a lazy eye). This certainly should be done before the child reaches seven years but it is best to have it investigated before kindergarten.

4   Eye exercises *may* help weak eye muscles but they do not help vision impairment.

5   Not every referral will result in the child's wearing glasses or submitting to other types of correction. The eye specialist must evaluate each case individually and prescribe only when it is needed. Some over-referral on this basis is still better than under-referral.

When a pupil continues to evidence one or a combination of the symptoms above under 3a following an eye exam that shows good "eyeball" vision, then the visual perception should be properly examined. Some school districts are visited by an eye survey team. Their check-ups are most helpful because their work is carried out under the direction of a professional.

The use of the Telebinocular or Titmus eye examination machines is useful and of greater value than the Snellen Chart test, if carried out by school nurses or school health personnel who are proficient in their use.

Eye specialists are by no means in agreement as to what tests or equipment should or should not be used in schools for routine eye examinations. Thus the best course of action is to find out the majority opinion of the eye specialists in your area who work best with children and then to follow their recommendations. In the article "On Research in Visual Training and Reading Disability" (Krippner 1971) the pros and cons of the issue are discussed.

Ear Examination

Two types of testing with special equipment are recommended.

1 *The Audiometer*   This machine checks each ear to determine how well a person hears the various frequencies of sound at various levels of intensity or volume. All grammar school children should have their hearing checked routinely with this machine at least twice during the years of their elementary school education.

Any test result which is not within normal limits should be repeated in about one week. If it still is abnormal, his parents should be informed and the child taken to a physician for a check-up and treatment or for further referral to an ear specialist, as the case may be.

Any physical problem such as acute or chronic infection, injury, wax plugging of the ear canal, sound conduction problem and other possible maladies will be treated. *But* if the child is returned with either no physical ear problems or with treated or corrected physical problems and yet his hearing problems at school and in the home continue, *then further hearing testing* is necessary in the areas of Auditory (hearing) Perception and Auditory Discrimination. The observable problems might be the child's inability to remember instructions the first time they are given . . . his need of higher volume to hear . . . or his inability to carry out apparently understood verbal instructions. The Auditory Discrimination tests will determine whether the patient can distinguish between different sounds or words that are almost alike or whether two similar sounds repeated are the same to that person.

Can a normal result with the audiometer be misleading? Further knowledge of brain function indicates that the hearing center of the right cerebral hemisphere of the brain is concerned mainly with non-verbal sounds—music, noises, tones, taps, clicks, etc. Whereas the center of the left side (usually the dominant hemisphere) is for verbal sounds—words spoken or sung. Thus a normal result with the audiometer simply indicates that the right hearing center is functioning with normal sound frequencies at adequate intensity (decibels) *BUT* it tells you nothing about the auditory function of the verbal hearing center on the left (Bogen and Gordon 1971, Bogen and Bogen 1969, and Bakan 1971).

Most children with learning problems in school have normal func-

tioning eyes and ears but their perceptual functioning is frequently impaired in one or both.

2   *The Wepman Auditory Discrimination Test*   This hearing test is one of several which tests a person's ability to distinguish between same or different sounds. Any child or adult whose hearing is suspect in relation to a learning problem should be examined with this or a comparable test.

Some students who have good ears and good perception still act as though they do not hear well. This imperception could be caused by overactivity of the nervous system, whether outwardly obvious or not. The trouble produces a short attention span so that what is heard or seen is not really grasped by the mind.

The ideal situation in any school system—public, private, religious or private secular—is the use of screening tests for every pupil entering the school either at kindergarten or first grade levels. Pupils beyond these grades would receive the testing only if they were having learning and/or behavior problems even to a minimal degree. The screening process would identify the problem areas early.

The basic function of the sense organs and how they relate to the brain can be better understood after viewing films on these subjects produced by the Moody Institute of Science, Whittier, California. Their film "Sense Perception" is the educational version of a film which has had wide usage in school districts across the nation and in foreign lands. The religious version of this film is called "Windows of the Soul" which can be obtained through distributors of church films. The religious version, which was the original one, adds a spiritual dimension to the scientific material presented.

The Psalmist (Psalms 139:14) wrote of more than he knew when he exclaimed in awe and thanksgiving to God: "I am fearfully and wonderfully made."

BIBLIOGRAPHY FOR CHAPTER SIX

Bakan, Paul, The Eyes Have It, *Psychology Today,* Vol. 4, No. 11, pp. 64-67, April, 1971

Bogen, Joseph E., and **Bogen,** Glenda M., The Other Side of the Brain III: The Corpus Callosum and Creativity, *The Bulletin of the Los Angeles Neurological Society,* Vol. 34, No. 4, October, 1969.

Bogen, Joseph E., and **Gordon,** Harold W., Musical Tests for Functional Lateralization with Intracarotid Amobarbital, *Nature,* Vol. 230, No. 5295, pp. 524-525, April 23, 1971.

Holy Bible (NAS) Psalms, chapter 139, verse 14, The Lockman Foundation, Creation House, Inc., Illinois, 1971.

Krippner, Stanley, Research in Visual Training and Reading Disability, *Journal of Learning Disabilities,* Vol. 4, No. 2, pp. 65-76, February, 1971.

CHAPTER SEVEN

THE BRAIN

Nothing in the human body functions without the direct or indirect supervision of the brain. Physical, emotional, intellectual, social or spiritual matters all are routed through that mysterious, "pint-sized" computer that rules each one of us.

Many people think of the brain only as sane or insane, intelligent or dull, expert in memory or forgetful. . . .

The brain is naturally involved in these matters, but it is also concerned with much more. In fact, *the brain influences the entire body.* It is the master control; it is the most complete computer in existence, controlling the growth and function of the hair, skin, nails, heartbeat, breathing, and right on through. Every conscious act is accomplished by the functioning of our brain. And every involuntary act carried out by our bodies without our conscious thought is also done under the control of the brain. The involuntary functions are under the control of the autonomic, or if you prefer the "automatic," portion of the nervous system and include such things as the production of blood, the digestion of food, the flow of the blood through all of the various vessels, the operation of every organ in the body.

For example, I may exert my own will and activate the voluntary part of my nervous system to decide how I will move a given set of muscles in order to write with my fingers and thumb. But on the other hand, the automatic or non-voluntary portion of my nervous system controls the flow of blood to those muscles and determines how each muscle cell maintains itself. Describing the brain as a computer is the best way to illustrate its function, but it is a great over simplification of its usage.

The average adult has an estimated thirty trillion cells in his body. Each one is under the direct or indirect control of the brain through hormones or other substances. All the various hormones of the body—thyroid hormone, adrenalin, sex determining hormones—are under the control of the master hormone gland—the Pituitary. This gland is connected to and under the control of the brain. The brain handles the trophic function of each cell thus controlling what it should take out of the blood stream, how it should use it, how to carry out its function and how its waste products are to be put back into the blood stream.

The cells of the brain, called neurons, number by conservative estimate fourteen billion. Each neuron has approximately twenty-five thousand connections called dendrites. Try to imagine the different combinations of connections available to the brain through fourteen billion cells and twenty-five thousand connections with each cell and you get a quick idea of the staggering complexity of this organ.

The brain operates on electrical-chemical energy. If you want to move your arm the brain sends electrical messages down the nerves to the various muscles and tells them how to function. While it is telling one muscle to contract, it tells an opposing muscle to relax, otherwise the moving part would stiffen. *This is an example of the physical control of the body which is under the direction of the brain.*

All physical sensation, conscious (aware) and subconscious (unaware), is sent to the brain. Through our five senses (seeing, hearing, touching, tasting, and smelling) plus other senses we are aware of the physical world about us. The physical body gives us a *world* consciousness. In order to provide adequate output control the brain must have good input sensory information. For example, muscles and joints are always informing the brain of their location and position. This is the proprioceptive and kinesthetic sense.

Are you aware of such messages arriving in the brain? Probably not. But if you fall in the dark from loss of balance then the accident is likely due to poor muscle and joint sense information or the improper interpretation of it by the brain.

The brain is not just flesh and blood, however. It is also the seat of the will of man. It is the location of the mind of man, the center of all his various emotions that have to do with the psychological aspects of life. Thus *the brain is the seat of the soul,* the self-consciousness of the human being.

Apart from the brain you could not love or hate, experience joy or sadness, worth or guilt, confidence or fear, peace or anxiety.

The brain is also *the seat of the spirit of man,* his consciousness of a greater power than his own . . . or a Supreme-Being consciousness. A God consciousness.

The Biblical reference I Corinthians 2:11 (Holy Bible) indicates that it is also the spirit of man that supplies his quality and capability of knowledge. "For who among men knows the thoughts of a man except the spirit of the man, which is in him?" The physical brain, controller of the body, gives the soul and spirit of man the ability to make vital contact with the physical world given to us by God to enjoy.

But since the brain is the master control center for the body, what controls the brain? The heart is similarly dependent. It pumps necessary life-sustaining blood to every part of the body but it too needs blood for its muscles, nerves and other tissues which it receives in the relaxing period between each beat. The brain is controlled by the soul and spirit, yet man is a whole being with body, soul and spirit all dependent upon each other. All are interrelated to make a person. This phenomenon is the neuro-pneumo-psycho-physiologic or somatic aspect of medicine, of human life. *Pneumo* refers to spirit, *psycho* to soul, and *physiologic* or *somatic* to body.

In this world we face problems of behavior, learning, and other dilemmas related to the function of the brain. The *physical function* is the subject of neurology; the *emotional function* of the brain is the subject of psychology; the *abnormal emotions* are the study of abnormal psychology and psychiatry. The last two involve a person's ego but when the problem is merely a neurological one this too can involve the ego.

For example, when parents bring to a specialist a child who is having either behavior problems or learning problems or both and they are told the youngster's brain is not functioning efficiently neurologically the diagnosis can result in an ego problem. The parents find it hard to accept the news that their child's brain is not functioning as it should. Imagine a teenager's reaction to the news that in this period of adjustment and maturing his brain function is not as it should be. The diagnosis insults his self-concept and damages his own self-image.

Thus it must be emphasized again and again that a neurological problem of the brain in no way specifically puts the person in the category either of being unintelligent or emotionally ill.

On the other hand, the longer a neurological problem is allowed to continue without proper diagnosis and adequate treatment, the greater the possibility of emotional problems developing in that person as a direct result of neurological insufficiencies. Through proper treatment, many a nervous, frustrating situation has been alleviated to some degree. The whole person has benefitted physically, psychologically and spiritually from proper treatment in time.

Some of these concepts concerning the brain may be new or startling—even incredible. But one thing all of us are ready to admit: The brain is the most complex organ in the human body. Even with his enormous capacity for research and development, man has only begun to comprehend the function of God's masterful creation called the brain.

The Brain— Cortical Areas of Conscious Function
View of the left side of the Left Cerebral (brain) Hemisphere.

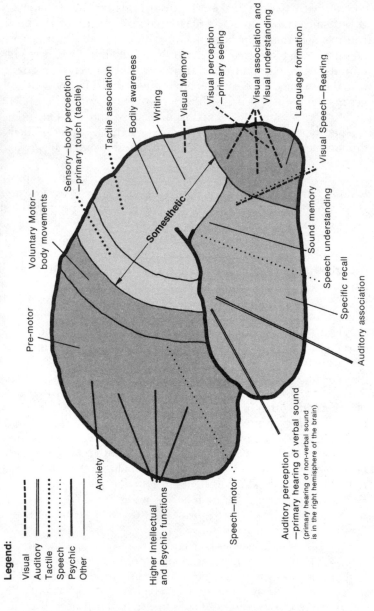

Legend:

Visual
Auditory
Tactile
Speech
Psychic
Other

The Brain– General Regions

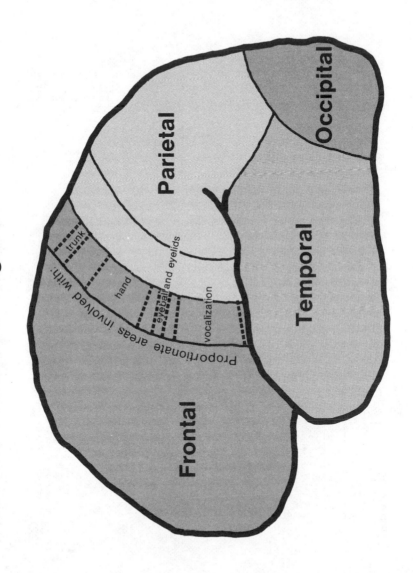

Frontal

Parietal

Occipital

Temporal

Proportionate areas involved with:

trunk

hand

eyeball and eyelids

vocalization

"HOW WE LEARN"—A SCHEMATIC

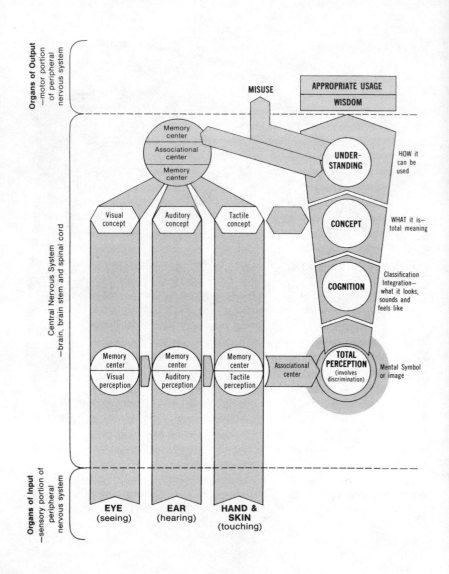

The schematic diagram "How We Learn" on page 50 offers assistance in gaining a clearer idea of the processes that take place in the brain in the learning mechanism.

A study of the diagram step by step will supply a better understanding of the learning process accomplished by the brain. This explanation will be by no means complete or exhaustive but it will provide an idea of the intricacies of the process.

Take, for example, a cat which you see for the first time with your eyes—either in real life or in a picture. The image is visually perceived in the brain and the information stored in the visual memory center. At this point there is nothing else to associate with it because this has been your first contact with a cat and it was silent.

That night you hear a noise in the back yard and you are told that it is the sound of a cat. Your ears pick up the sound which is perceived in the auditory portion of the brain, stored in the adjacent memory center for hearing and in the association center for hearing that interrelates with the association center for vision because you were told the sound applied to a cat which you had seen earlier.

The following day a visitor arrives bringing a cat to your house. You are allowed to touch the cat with your hand. Through the touch or tactile perception you get an idea how a cat feels—fur, whiskers, tail, feet, etc., and all this reinforces your visual perceptual memory center. As you stroke the cat it purrs and adds further auditory information to the auditory perceptual memory center and the association centers that interrelate with hearing and vision. Then you are well on your way to obtaining a complete mental image of what a cat is like.

As you enjoy the cat, your friend and parents tell you that it is an animal, a pet, a playmate you can enjoy. You learn that you must treat it in a certain way or it may misbehave—and now you are into the area of cognition. You learn that although the cat breathes and eats and walks that it is not a human being, although it has functions similar to human beings.

As you see and play more and more with this cat and additional cats your total concept of the cat develops. You note how agile it is, how it can run, jump and make horrible noises to scare off dogs and other unwanted animals. And one day you pull too hard on its tail and get a stinging scratch from a sharp claw. All this (visual, auditory and tactile) means your concept of the animal is becoming full-orbed. All this time your understanding of the animal has been developing so that you know how the animal can be used. The understanding is positive because you have learned by experience as well as by the information from others how you can wisely get along with a cat and enjoy it. This is wisdom. You also understand how you may harm the animal and lose its friendship temporarily or permanently. This is misuse.

A period of time may pass in which you see no cats. But should someone mention the name "cat," should you see a picture of a cat, or should you simply hear a cat's meow, your various visual, auditory and tactile memory and associational centers would bring to your specific recall center in the temporal area of your brain the features of a cat which you had previously learned. Each new contact or association with the cat will either reinforce previous perceptual, cognitive and conceptual information or add new information in these areas so that your understanding will be strengthened as well as enlarged concerning a cat.

Let us thank God for the empires of our minds, and for the pleasures they allow. And let us also remind ourselves that the malfunction of the brain is not a shameful thing, but something which can be treated and hopefully remedied if caught in the supple years of youth.

BIBLIOGRAPHY FOR CHAPTER SEVEN

Chalfant, J. C., and **Scheffelin,** M. A., Central Processing Dysfunctions in Children: A Review of Research, *NINDS* Monograph No. 9, U.S. Department of Health, Education and Welfare, Bethesda, Md., 1969.

Chusid, Joseph G., M.D., and **McDonald,** Joseph J., M.D., *Correlative Neuroanatomy and Functional Neurology,* 12th Edition, Lange Medical Publications, Los Altos, California, 1964.

Gregory, R. L., *Eye and Brain:* The Psychology of Seeing, World University Library, McGraw-Hill Book Company, New York, 1966.

Holy Bible (NAS), First Corinthians, chapter 2, verse 11, The Lockman Foundation, Creation House, Inc., Illinois, 1971.

Wooldridge, Dean E., Research Associate, California Institute of Technology, *The Machinery of the Brain,* McGraw-Hill Book Co., New York, 1963.

CHAPTER EIGHT

ONLY SPECIALISTS SHOULD TEST

The popular "EKG" reveals the electrical function of the heart. The not-as-popular "EEG" (electroencephalogram) tests the electrical function of the brain. This fascinating computer at the center of the human nervous system tells us a lot about itself in this and in other sophisticated neurological tests.

In the study of learning disabilities the EEG is one of many important tests, just as it is in the study of neurology. According to Dorland's Medical Dictionary, 24th Edition, neurology is "that branch of medical science which deals with the nervous system, both normal and in disease."

"The Nervous System," Dorland continues, is "the chief organ system which correlates the adjustments and reactions of an organism to internal and environmental conditions. It comprises *the central and peripheral nervous systems:* The former is composed of *the brain and spinal cord,* and the latter includes all the other neural elements." The main one among these elements is the autonomic nervous system which can also be called the non-voluntary portion of the whole nervous system.

A neurological examination checks the nervous system to determine if it is functioning properly. This system, as stated in the previous chapter, controls the function of every part and process of the entire body.

A very important aspect of that function is *learning.* When this process is checked with the *usual* neurological examination on obviously healthy pupils who are underachieving in learning it is surprising to note that it reveals only a small amount of information that is helpful. These results are often called "soft" neurological signs. Lauretta Bender says, "The concept of 'soft' neurological signs is derived from the work of Paul Schilder and myself. The term applies specifically to neurologic deviations that occur in childhood development disorders, maturational lags, childhood schizophrenia, and the developmental dyslexias. The term does not refer to a mild or borderline neurologic sign" (Bender 1968). To the author, a "soft sign" refers to such things as fine motor coordination and balance dysfunction and could also refer to difficulties in the integration and the processing of sensory stimuli received by the central nervous system (Meier 1971). A "sign" is what a physician observes when examining a patient as contrasted to a symptom which is what a patient tells the physician about how the patient feels or acts.

Why is the usual neurological examination of limited value in searching for signs related to learning?

Richmond S. Paine, M.D., formerly of Children's Hospital in Washington, D.C., commented: "Perhaps as often as not the physician detects no definite abnormalities by even the careful neurological examination contemplated above unless in terms of an observation of hectic behavior or hyperactivity or shortness of attention. More definite documentation of an organic cerebral problem can often be obtained by the use of certain tests which overlap the field of Neurology and Psychology" (Paine 1965).

Elena Boder, M.D., Pediatric Neurologist, also speaks of this subject: "An expanded neurological examination for the detection of minimal or so-called 'soft' neurologic signs is performed on all children, since the routine conventional neurological examination often reveals no abnormalities in children with minimal brain . . . dysfunction" (Boder 1966).

Dr. Boder goes on to say that, "The expanded examination consists of items from the conventional neurological examination, elaborated to achieve greater sensitivity to minimal signs, and adaptations of certain tests shared by the field of neurology, psychology and education."

In the Neurological and Sensory Disease Control Program monograph (Clements 1969), the following statement is made:

"Conventional neurological examination is heavily weighted in testing noncortical regions, i.e., spinal cord, brain stem, cerebellum, basal ganglia, primary motor and sensory pathways and peripheral nerves. Since it is important in minimal brain dysfunction to have more information concerning behavioral and cognitive function, the examination has been appropriately modified."

This has also been the experience of the author. In the mid 1960s the usual neurological exam was performed, but since then much of it has been modified or replaced by an examination designed to point out as specifically as possible the types or kinds of misfunction directly or indirectly responsible for underachievement in education.

The general underlying causes of learning problems are listed in chapter five. But in chapter three, page 23, there appear under "Diagnoses" in the right hand column some of the specific diagnoses which denote the area of misfunction. In some of these "Specific Diagnoses" the correct type of examination will further point out a more precise item of misfunction.

For example, there is the specific diagnosis of "Visual Perceptual Problem," but tests can further delineate what part of visual perception is involved. It may be a "figure-ground" problem or a "form constancy" problem, etc.

The balance of this chapter will take the form of questions and answers and abbreviated outline in our continuing consideration of neurology as it relates to the search for causes of learning disabilities.

What value is a routine physical examination for children with learning problems?

This question must be carefully considered, because it has caused misunderstanding and even ill feeling between physicians and educators—including school psychologists.

Here is a case in point: Bobby is an underachieving third grader. He's quite overactive and disturbs the class more often than not. The school has kept the parents informed of the problem and of the various educational, psychological and disciplinary ways it is using to try to remedy the situation.

Some days bring hope (because Bobby is trying his best, whether others think so or not) and other days shatter all hope of good behavior. Finally, after trying all available means, the school authorities suggest that a physical cause for Bobby's overactivity should be checked out.

The parents take their healthy boy to the family physician. After a thorough general physical examination the physician pronounces him quite healthy. Although Bobby remains overactive, nothing turned up in the exam to indicate the cause of it or to serve as a clue to the reason for his learning disability.

The physician is not as frustrated as the parents and the educators or as puzzled as the child who, deep inside, yearns for release from his shackles. Tensions begin to rise as the matter is discussed with the doctor. He has been asked to look for something in which he has little knowledge or training (Wender and Eisenberg 1971, Colodny, Kenny and Kurlander 1968). He is over-extended in his regular busy practice so there isn't time to learn about new approaches to Bobby's type of problem. The school and the parents become up-tight because the doctor was of little help in the matter.

The infrequent physical inadequacies that interfere with learning can be picked up on a routine physical examination. They have to do with the visual acuity of the eyes and the ability of the ears to hear. Often, but not always, children with such eye and ear problems have been treated successfully for those maladies before the learning problem became apparent.

Glandular or hormonal problems are sometimes cited as physical causes of learning difficulties. These may indeed be the culprits in a few cases. Physicians can easily check these out when confronted with symptoms and signs indicating hormonal problems.

A *Basic Principle* can be attached to routine physical examinations: When a physical condition (eye, ear, hormonal, etc.) is found to exist in children with learning problems, do not accept that as the only cause unless proper neurological and perceptual testing has turned out to be within normal limits.

It is quite normal for physicians who are confronted with a problem that extends beyond their training to refer their patient to a specialist. But referral to a neurologist should be accompanied by the information that the patient has a learning problem and needs the supervision of someone trained in this specialty. A good physical examination for an underachieving child is the first step if there is any question about his health status. The prescribed treatment for any deficiencies such as anemia, low thyroid or high thyroid, undernourishment (many youngsters load up on sweets and starches and rob their bodies of proper vitamins, minerals and protein because there are too few greens, fruits, vegetables and meat in their diet), or whatever the trouble, should be conscientiously carried out.

Is the neurological examination prescribed only for the overactive child with a learning problem?

The wheel that squeaks the loudest gets the grease. It's that way with underachievers. Loud troublemakers are usually singled out for assistance ahead of the quiet plodders who often need help just as desperately. Therefore the basic principle of operation is that *any* student who is underachieving, whether overactive or not, should have a neurological examination designed for such problems.

A quiet, "bump-on-a-log" pupil can have the same neurological perceptual deficits that characterize an overactive pupil. If that seems strange, read the principle again because it is terribly important. Medication and corrective measures are not only designed for the overactive patients but can be useful in the treatment of any underachiever as well. This basic principle is enlarged upon in the treatment chapters.

How are the various neurological examinations evaluated?

Such tests are measured in two ways. One involves specific measurements which fall within the normal range or which do not. The second involves a measurement based on the physician's clinical judgment as to whether something is within normal limits or not. His judgment is based upon training and experience gained through medical practice. On the basis of these he determines whether results from a test are significant or not.

The test may involve only the physician's hands, eyes and ears, or he may use a simple instrument such as a light or reflex hammer. He may also use a difficult or involved test such as a blood hormone test or even the Electroencephalogram (EEG or brain wave test).

The science of medicine, general and specialized, is more an art than an exact science like mathematics. Therefore, even when up-to-date scientific diagnostic tools and tests are available the more specific data must be judged clinically to determine if it has direct or indirect meaning and relevance to the problem of the patient.

What should the neurological examination for learning problems include?

Basically, such an exam should include tests or observations which show the presence or absence of the items listed on pages 57 to 63. Even though it sounds basic, academic and obvious, it is important to note that if the specialist does not test for a given item he will never know whether or not it is present and if present, whether it is functioning properly.

For example, the physician cannot assume that because a patient is twelve years old that he knows his right from his left. He must test for it, even though the difference between right and left is usually comprehended correctly by the age of seven years. Observations are meaningful only if the one observing notes the presence or absence of a critical factor. For example, a child may not appear to be grossly overactive but subtle signs of hyperactivity during the examination should be noted such as fine tremors of the eyelids when closed or of the tongue when extended. Other signs may be tightly squeezed eyelids or tremors of the hands or arms when extended, or when the movements of body parts such as arms and legs are performed either with much gusto or very rapidly, with little concern for accuracy, etc. When any of these idiosyncracies are revealed by the examinations the specialist knows that overactivity or hyperkinesis is present.

Testing should include the search for:

1   *Right and Left Reversal and/or Confusion (directionality)*
    "Confusion" is characteristic of a child who is not certain of right and

Learning Neurological Comparisons

Test Item—number corresponds to text	Achievers N=33 #	Achievers N=33 %	Underachievers N=34 #	Underachievers N=34 %	Aphasics N=9 or 14* #	Aphasics N=9 or 14* %
1 · Right and Left reversals						
a. Tongue		6.1		20.6		66.7
b. Gross Body Perception—verbal		0.0		38.2		44.4
c. Finger to Nose		3.0		29.4		22.2
d. Fine Tactile Perception		9.0		41.2		22.2
Average errors per person	4.66		7.07		2.50	
2 · Dominance						
a. Eye-Ear mixed**		36.4		64.7		78.5*
b. All Right dominant (eye-ear-hand-foot)		36.4		24.2		0*
c. All Left dominant		0		0		0*
d. Eye-hand Right		39.4		20.6		42.8*
e. Eye-hand Left		0		0		7.1*
f. Eye-hand Mixed***		60.6		79.4		50.0*
3 · Tongue movements						
a. Flexion		0		17.6		33.3
b. Extension		0		2.9		22.2
c. Side to side		Not done		Not done		77.8
d. Rapid "t"		0		26.5		88.9
e. Tremor		30.3		54.5		33.3
6 · Coordination						
a. Finger-Nose						
Eyes open		9.0		57.6		
Eyes shut		57.6		97.0		
b. Finger thumb****		75.6		94.1		100.0
average error per person	1.12		2.15		5.11	

Interpretation or Comments

**Few are aware of this significance.

***Not a significant finding in learning disabilities as so many think.

****Note the difference in errors per person, the degree of error, or length of time as well as the percentages.

	Group 1		Group 2		Group 3	
average pluses per person	1.08		2.75		3.11	
c. Hand reversals**** average pluses per person	1.00	60.6	1.88	94.1	2.77	100.0
7 · Balance-single foot						
a. Eyes open****	6.1		24.2		88.9	
	Right	Left	Right	Left	Right	Left
10 second average	10	9.85	9.10	8.80	6.5	5.75
15 second average	14.85	15	14.69	14.54	8.4	10.0
b. Eyes shut****	63.6		97.0		100.0	
10 second average	7.57	7.57	3.80	5.10	2.5	1.75
15 second average	14.00	12.61	9.61	8.69	2.4	3.4
8 · Gross body perception						
a. Verbal regular*****	21.2		50.0		66.7	
crossovers	51.5		70.6		66.7	
b. Tactile regular	72.7		82.3		77.8	
crossovers	78.8		82.3		77.8	
9 · Fine tactile perception****	69.7		84.8		75.0	
number of errors	40		77		21	
average errors per person	1.73		2.75		3.50	
12a · Hyperactivity	9.0		50.0		38.5	
12 · Persistence tests — Average Time	N = 9		N = 8		N = 7	
a. Get up fast	1.83	33.3	1.65	25.0	2.54	42.9
b. Get up slow	19.58	0	7.25	50.0	6.32	57.1
c. Draw 12-inch line slow	99.13	44.4	30.35	87.5	15.58	100.0
d. Walk 12-foot line slow	83.74	44.4	18.92	100.0	13.22	100.0
12d · Alternating right and left with same command	0		3.0		44.4	
Concentration	39.4		44.1		66.7	

*****If one cannot relate verbal symbols with large parts of their own physical body, then one would assume that it would be more difficult to relate verbal symbols with their environment.

N—stands for the number of persons that were tested.

left directions but who gets it correct eventually in a given test. This observation is checked during the tongue movement, finger-to-nose application, finger identification, and gross body perception tests.

2 *Mixed Dominance*

Most dominance testing involves only the eye and the hand. Some include the foot. But ear dominance is rarely tested in this procedure, although it should be every time.

Mixed eye-hand dominance is not significant in learning problems (Bettman, Stern, Whitzell and Gofman 1967, and Harris, Otto, Barrett and Mattingly 1968). Besides, it is comparing the eye—an intake sensory organ—with the hand—an output motor organ basically, although it does involve intake sensory functions (touch or "tactile") as well.

Adequate dominance testing should concentrate on eye and ear dominance and should also include hand and foot dominance.

3 *Tongue Movements*

This test involves the extending of the tongue out straight, the flexion of the tongue toward the nose, extension toward the chin, and rapid repetitive movements required in pronouncing the letter "t" quickly and clearly and making the tongue go rapidly from side to side within the mouth with the mouth partly open for observation.

4 *Eye Convergence*

This test determines if the eyes converge adequately to the near point.

5 *Eye Fusion*

By using the AO 4 Dot Test, the specialist checks the eyes at eight inches and twenty-four inches. He checks also any suppression of vision, be it total or intermittent, in either eye.

The table on pages 58 and 59 indicates the relative merit of some of these tests as they are compared with achievers, underachievers and aphasics.

6 *Fine Motor Coordination*

Precise finger-to-nose, finger-to-thumb and rapid hand reversal movements (diadokokinesis) tests are difficult to do by most underachievers.

7 *Single Foot Balance*

This test is performed on each foot of the patient, first with his eyes open and then with his eyes closed. For most underachievers it is not possible to stand the required time on one foot with their eyes shut. Why their balance by proprioceptive kinesthetic sense (muscle and joint position) is impaired is not known (Kohen-Raz 1970).

8 *Gross Body Perception*

By using verbal commands, then by touch, and finally by visual cues, these tests measure how well the patient knows his arms and legs with his eyes shut, including proper knowledge of the right or left side.

9 *Fine Touch Perception or Finger Identification Test*

With eyes closed, the examiner touches each digit separately in random fashion (fingers and thumbs) to reveal if the patient can declare them accurately and if he knows left from right.

10 *Tactile (touch) Perception of Single Objects and Discrimination of Two Objects*

With eyes closed, the patient receives an object in one hand or one object in each hand at the same time and names the objects, each hand working independently.

11 *Reading Direction*

A special "Reading Direction Test" has been developed by the author on behalf of young patients. Parts one, two and three of the test are designed to see if the pupil properly understands and carries out the concept of the word "read." In our part of the world this means one crosses the page horizontally from left to right. This is a learned procedure and many of us forget that about half the world's population reads in the opposite fashion—from right to left and vertically (e.g., Chinese, Japanese and other Asiatics). The Hebrews, to provide another example, read also from right to left but horizontally as do readers of English. Part four of the test checks for reversals of letters, words and numbers, as well as for letter or word exchanges.

The "Reading Direction Test" is being readied for use by those specialists who are working in the area of learning disabilities.

12 *Hyperactivity*

This trait can be assessed by using a stop watch in the patient's performance of drawing a 12-inch line slowly, getting up slowly and walking a 12-foot line slowly. Bryant Cratty has some data on the walking part. He calls these "persistence tests" (Cratty and Martin 1970).

Testing for such keyed-up tensions includes observations checking for the following:

a. *Hyperkinesis (Hyperactivity or Overactivity)*

This characteristic can be either grossly obvious or subtly hidden. Therefore, careful observation must make note of tremors of tongue, closed eyelids, extended arms, hands and fingers, or excessive use of energy in the performance of routine tasks.

Note: Although a patient may be well behaved in the doctor's office, that doesn't mean the patient is *not* hyperactive. His teacher and parents usually have good reasons to report overactivity. Different environments, such as the home, the school, the doctor's office, the neighborhood, etc., affect people in different ways. A kid who "climbs the walls" at home might be able to muster all available control factors when he's in the doctor's office. He might fear a "shot" or figure he'll miss out on a lollipop if he doesn't behave correctly. He might even put into play the law of "cussedness," doing the opposite that's intended or suspected. Like the auto engine that plagues you with noise until it's in the mechanic's shop then purrs like a kitten until you're back home again.

b. *Perseveration*

Dorland's Medical Dictionary defines this phenomenon as the "continuance of any activity after cessation of the causative stimulus." This is demonstrated when a patient is told on command during the Gross Body Perception test to raise and immediately lower a particular arm or leg and then lets the arm or leg remain up for a while instead of lowering it immediately or when he holds his finger on the end of his nose for a period of time rather than just touching it quickly in the Finger-to-Nose test. All this points to "Perseveration."

Although it interferes with the function of children with normal IQ, Perseveration can be used to great advantage on behalf of those in retarded IQ ranges as they are trained to carry out job functions requiring continuous repetitive acts, such as assembly-line work and other routine activity.

c. *Response to Verbal Commands*

This testing asks: Does the patient carry out verbal orders without having them repeated? Does he repeat the command quietly or just mouth it? Does he finally have to be shown? Does he use a trial-and-error method to accomplish a command? How many commands can he follow in one directive? Does he also confuse up from down, top from bottom, back from front in addition to his inability to determine right and left directions?

d. *Alternating Movements with the Same Command*

When the doctor asks the patient to touch the tip of the nose with the right or left index finger, does the patient keep bringing in the same side with alternating commands of "right side," "left side"? Or does he alternate sides when the command for the same side is repeated a few times? These are observations made in this phase of testing. If alternating is observed, auditory discrimination testing should be done.

e. *Comprehension and Cooperation*

These twin observations should be discussed at the end of the examination. Most pupils with learning problems do quite well in both comprehension and cooperation. But remember: During the examination they were working on a one-to-one basis, enjoying the examiner's constant attention in an area where there were few distractions. Such a situation is quite different from the classroom experience! Besides, the doctor told them the tests were not for passing or for failing—just to find out how things were functioning. This helps the underachiever to feel accepted, and he needs such reassurance in abundant measure.

The neurological examination for learning problems varies with physicians, both in the type of test and in the technique for administering it. A couple of examples are listed at the end of this chapter.(Fuisz and Fuisz 1971, Rabe 1969).

Some tests available to doctors today have been developed by people in non-medical professions (Ayres 1968).

Various doctors have developed learning neurological exams, some of which are available upon request. The author would be happy to share his upon request.

Is the Electroencephalogram—EEG—Brain Wave Test useful in the care of these patients?

A complete EEG exam properly carried out by a trained, experienced technician, a test which is adequately interpreted and reported upon by a qualified physician with results correlated with the clinical picture of the patient with the learning problem, can be helpful in making a diagnosis (Gross and Wilson 1964).

The usefulness of the EEG has been brought into sharper focus by Eeg Olofsson, Petersen, and Sellden (1971). They performed complete physicals and EEG workups on 743 children, of which 389 were female and 284 male. The age range was one to 15 years.

The children examined were well screened for pregnancy and birth difficulties, trauma and illness, and also for any school and/or emotional problems. The subjects were as normal as possible. The astounding conclusion is that the examiners found a very small percentage with abnormal EEGs. Only 2.7 per cent had paroxysmal activity at rest (1.9 per cent had focal spikes or sharp waves; 0.5 per cent had focal spike-like activity; 0.3 per cent had paroxysmal slow activity). Note: *only 0.3 per cent* had slow wave paroxysms! During hyperventilation paroxysmal activity was noticed in 0.3 per cent, during intermittent photic stimulation in 9.1 per cent.

Certain abnormalities in the tracing can serve as a guide to medication.

The Electroencephalogram . . . EEG . . . Brain Wave Test—all are synonymous terms. The EEG is a study of the electrical activity and electrical pattern of the brain which functions on electrical-chemical energy. It is a different type of electricity than that used for running our lights and electrical appliances. Household electricity can kill a person, but the electricity in our brains causes our bodies to function in thousands of ways. These functions are carried on by the brain's electricity either directly or through other electrical biochemical means. Thus, we emphasize the fact that when a person has an EEG the technician is measuring *only* the electrical activity in terms of the frequency (in cycles per second), the amount (in microvolts) and the electrical pattern of the brain. IT IS IN NO WAY A MEASUREMENT OF INTELLIGENCE OR SANITY OR ANYTHING ELSE OTHER THAN AS STATED ABOVE.

Some studies were done by Dr. Ertl (1968) who found a possible correlation between brain wave response (EEG) to a flash of light and intelligence (IQ).

Many people are familiar with the EKG (electrocardiogram) for measuring the *heart's electrical pattern*. This is based on the same principle, except that we are measuring the *brain's* pattern instead. There are also machines for measuring the electrical pattern of muscle action. Everytime you move a muscle it is moving because an electrical stimulus which originated in the central nervous system and travelled over a nerve activates the muscle. The brain never stops working while a person is alive; thus, there is an electrical pattern being put out from all the various areas of the brain, at all times, whether a person is awake or asleep.

The EEG machine is a very sensitive electronic instrument which picks up the electrical impulses of the brain through the wires that are attached to a person's scalp. Nothing is felt during the test, and there is nothing put into the person. Only the electrical current coming off the person's brain and head are picked up by these wires and amplified through the machine so that tracings can be recorded on paper. An up-to-date EEG lab will just glue the electrode wires to the scalp with a special paste which is easily removed. There are some labs that still use pins that are actually inserted into the scalp, but such discomfort for the patient, either child or adult, is not really necessary.

The EEG is only one of many ways of measuring the brain in its varied and numerous functions. Like any test, the EEG does not establish or cancel out a given diagnosis. It is only one part of the whole picture in evaluating the possibility of a person's having a neurological problem. A high percentage of diagnoses for any medical problem is made from an adequate history of that problem in a given patient. Physical and neurological and other exams plus lab tests are used to confirm further the correct diagnosis.

The EEG has its limitations because a person can have definite clinical evidence of a neurological problem and still have a normal-appearing EEG record. Such cases are infrequent. It can also be stated that there are those who have no clinical symptoms or signs of a neurological problem, and yet have an abnormal brain-wave tracing. This only further emphasizes the necessity for obtaining full and complete information from every reasonable avenue available, and making a diagnosis from the complete picture of the problem and not from just one aspect of it.

The EEG machine is one of the best we have for obtaining an electrical pattern of the brain. It is a wonderful instrument and has been a help to many. On the other hand, it must be remembered that measuring the brain electrically with the EEG machine is probably compared to measuring North America accurately with a 100-yard tape measure.

Here is an idea of what is involved. The brain has 14 billion cells and by actual count the average nerve cell, called a "neuron," has on the average approximately 25,000 connections called "dendrites." This gives us a little idea of the complexity of this master control computer which each person has, and how, basically speaking, the present day instruments for measuring brain function are only a small beginning. Nevertheless, it is wonderful to be able to use this knowledge from present technology to the best of our abilities to help those who are having specific problems and are seeking help.

What do the results of an EEG mean?

When the EEG is reported as being "normal" one must realize that in most medical tests there is a *range of normal*. Thus, an EEG can be completely normal and raise no suspicion at all that any abnormal pattern exists. On the other hand, it may be normal with a few abnormal patterns in the tracing, but the recurrence or the extent of the abnormal patterns is not sufficient to classify the tracing as abnormal.

Next, an EEG can be "borderline." This term speaks for itself. It also can be "abnormal" and the abnormalities can be divided into several grades. One such division has five different grades or degrees of abnormality. The lower grade is borderline, the second grade minimal, and up to grade five which is termed "severe." Here again, it is well to state that severity, or the lack of it, in the EEG tracing may not always fully correlate with the severity or lack of it as far as the patient's total problem is concerned. There is often fairly good correlation between the two but not always.

The EEG tracing is helpful in determining what type of medicine may be most advantageous. That is to say, the various types of abnormal patterns that can be found in the EEG tracing are known, by experience, to respond better to certain medicines than to other medicines. Thus, several types of abnormal patterns, one might say, have a "hit parade" of medicine and thus should be used first. Here again, though, it must be emphasized that the EEG alone does not direct the medication to be used. In the same way, it is not the only source for the diagnosis. There are indications in the medical-neurological picture of the learning problem which also aid in the choice of medications. Even though a certain medicine may be the medicine of choice for a certain pattern, no medicine works 100 per cent of the time in the condition for which it may be primarily indicated. We are fortunate in this modern scientific age to have a wide selection of medications from which we see a high percentage of effectiveness. Further discussion is set forth in the chapter on medications.

Any test, including the EEG, is only as good as the person who runs it and the person who interprets it. An EEG must be properly run. By this we mean that if a patient is having certain problems with sleep, this person may well have a normal EEG but such an EEG would be classified as inconclusive if a sleep pattern was not obtained. That is to say, the abnormality in such a case may not show up except when the person is asleep, or becoming drowsy or coming out of sleep (arousal), because the awake pattern of the EEG is different from the sleep pattern. Also, all of our brains are more unstable when we go from the "awake" to the "asleep" or from the "sleep" to "awake" pattern. There are also children with definite reading problems who develop certain physical symptoms while reading, and thus must be tested with a reading pattern during their EEG examination. Although it may be hard to believe, yet it is true that in some patients this stimulus of reading gives sufficient stress to the brain to produce an abnormal pattern (Oettinger, Nekonishi and Gill 1967). This alone can give us tremendous insight into the complexity and super-sensitivity of this amazing organ, the brain, which God has created and given to us. Thus, it is of utmost importance when an EEG is ordered that the correct testing items be requested and that they be carried out by the technician so that as conclusive results as possible may best be obtained through this medium.

For such problems the EEG should certainly include a period of hyperventilation, that is, when the person forcefully breathes heavily in and out, for this acts as a stress to the brain. We should also include photic stimulation which is a light with varying frequencies which also acts as a stress stimulus to the brain. Then a sleep pattern, which should be routine on every patient as far as it is practical.

There are still many unknown answers to the numerous questions regarding the EEG and its correlation to clinical problems. Constant research is being carried out to learn more about how we may more efficiently use its results.

Practical instructions from the EEG

If an EEG pattern fluctuates abnormally from hyperventilation, this shows that the patient is more apt to be upset at the end of physical activity. Thus, recess or gym for a child in school with this pattern should be cut short 5 or 10 minutes. The added time will allow him additional time to settle down before starting his next class.

This type of child, or even adult, is more apt to get into a verbal scrap or physical fight when he has been physically exerting himself, which normally should only result in heavy breathing.

When the photic stimulation produces an abnormal tracing indicating that bright light (whether sun or artificial) can act as an abnormal stimulus to the brain, the patient should do his work and his studying in a position where there is *no direct light into his eyes* or *reflected light.*

Parents who have children with the above mentioned items, either one or the other or both, should be sure to have their physician communicate this information to the teacher, or those concerned, so that proper steps may be carried out to improve the child's situation.

What is the percentage possibility of an abnormal EEG in pupils with learning problems?

Those with only a learning problem have a 50 to 70 per cent chance of having an abnormal pattern (Klinkerfuss, Lange, Weinberg and O'Leary 1965, Stevens, Sachdev, and Milstein 1968, and Torres and Ayres 1968). Most of the abnormalities seen by the author have been of the minimal type of grade two out of a possible five.

There are those who would disregard the results of an abnormal EEG in a patient with learning problems on the basis that a high percentage of those mentally ill and criminals (Williams 1969, Small 1966) have abnormal EEGs. The facts of those electrical brain tracings should not be discarded. Further inquiry and search should be made to see if the electrical dysfunction of the brain as indicated by the EEG had anything to do with the initial or primary cause of that person's problem or if it was an aggravating secondary process which helped only to worsen the total process that produces the mentally ill and the criminal. The author is persuaded that such is the case in a fair percentage of mental and criminal problems.

Headaches are fairly common among those with a learning disability. A study on headache in childhood by Kock and Melchior (1969) showed that 33 per cent had abnormal EEGs.

Dr. Small (1968) points out a distinction between the mentally ill with abnormal EEGs and the mentally ill with normal EEGs. Those with the abnormal EEGs had a higher incidence of speech and visual defects, enuresis, hyperactivity, destructive behavior, and impaired coordination.

Does an abnormal EEG pattern indicate Epilepsy, or a convulsive or a seizure problem?

It should be stated emphatically that an abnormal EEG pattern of itself does not indicate Epilepsy or the other two abnormalities. This was partially discussed in Chapter 3, page 22. Epileptic, convulsive, and seizure problems are diagnosed and identified specifically depending upon what the patient experienced during the convulsion or seizure or "fit" and what was observed if someone else was present. The EEG can supply additional laboratory information but it does not have the last word in making the diagnosis. It should be clearly stated that the EEG is never diagnostic.

It is generally accepted that about eight per cent of those with Grand Mal Epilepsy have normal EEGs on repeated examinations. Children who have convulsive seizures are observed in 75 to 85 per cent of cases to have paroxysmal abnormalities evident in their EEGs during the interseizure period (Farmer 1964). Therefore, 15 to 25 per cent have an EEG free of that abnormality. Thus a normal EEG should not cause one to conclude that there is no neurological problem.

By the same token, there are those who have never had any kind of convulsion or seizure and yet their EEGs show an abnormal pattern which classically goes with a certain type of seizure problem, namely Petit Mal, but they do not have Petit Mal Epilepsy!

Dr. Walter C. Alvarez (1969), in a concise editorial on enuresis (bedwetting), refers to several studies that bring out the high rate of abnormal EEGs among enuretics.

Diagnosis in any field or specialty of medicine is based on the total clinical picture which includes laboratory information but rarely on the result of a single test.

When the total clinical picture indicates that the brain of the pupil with the learning problem is not functioning properly, how does one explain this to the patient and parents?

The author has found that by using the analogy of a car that this communicates quite well.

The overactive or hyperactive child can be likened to a new automobile in which all normal parts are well synchronized with one difficulty: the accelerator, or throttle, is stuck. Every time the car functions it does so at a high speed. Sixty-five miles an hour is perfectly all right on the freeway, provided the other cars and trucks are going at the same speed; but if the other vehicles are going much more slowly, such as at rush hour, sixty-five miles an hour is going to bring problems. And try to leave the freeway at sixty-five miles an hour! This is virtually impossible.

One can also explain to these parents and the patient that it's pretty difficult to park a car even at five and ten miles an hour. To go around a corner at forty-five miles an hour is most dangerous for the occupant of the car and for anyone else who might be around that corner.

In daily life, whether in school or elsewhere, our bodies, minds, and the learning process require different speeds at different times for different functions or for similar functions under different circumstances. In any case, a car or a child who is running and functioning at a high speed or even at the same speed all the time is bound to run into difficulties.

Other children with learning problems may not necessarily be hyperactive and have an accelerator stuck at a high speed, but they may have the various perceptual problems or spacial orientation problems such as right and left, front and back, etc. These can be likened to a car that is new with new parts but these parts have not been tuned properly so that they work together simultaneously or synchronously. A car that is not tuned up is going to waste gas. It's not going to be able to operate at proper speeds and any time you try to get the car to go faster by accelerating, the car only further sputters and sputs, finally coming to a halt. In some cases the car even functions slower, and this is a good description of how many of these children work.

Often you find that they are referred to as "slow learners." As long as they go slowly they learn fairly well, but as soon as any pressure is applied on them by teacher, principal, or parents, they slow down even further and in some cases completely fall apart with a temper tantrum or in some other demonstrable means show their frustration under pressure. Many of these students are both overactive and out of tune, creating an even more frustrating misfunctioning situation.

What answer or explanation should be given to a parent whose child has an abnormal EEG and who asks, "Is my child brain injured or brain damaged?" It should be first explained to the parents and to the child that the terms "injured" and "damaged" are difficult for one's inner feelings to handle. Thus reference to a car that is going too fast and that has parts that are out of tune serves to illustrate that such a car, although misfunctioning, is not damaged or injured and that likewise the child's brain could be similarly misfunctioning.

In order to be scientifically accurate and clinically accurate it would be necessary for such a child to have in his or her past history an incident of trauma or accident to the brain or a specific disease such as meningitis or other conditions which produced damage or injury as evidenced by a definite change in the child's physical, emotional and mental behavior before and after the incident. Children with learning problems with such incidents as this are rare in the author's experience. Even for those who have a past medical history of such a specific problem it is also important to protect the ego of the child and the parents and to minimize and even completely avoid the usage of the terms "brain injury" and "brain damage" in order to take as positive a viewpoint as possible in the rehabilitation and treatment of such a child. It's bad having the problem but it's worse when those about you keep reminding you of it.

Thus it should be emphasized that the word "epilepsy" and the terms "brain injured" and "brain damaged" should be avoided as much as possible. It is best that they never be used in these children with learning disorders.

Those who insist on using the terms "injured" and "damaged" should look at themselves and very quickly and logically realize that all of us are basically brain damaged or injured! None of us is even beginning to use the mental capacity of his brain, also why is it that people are right handed or left handed? Why can we not use equally as well our two extremities? One could go on and on describing many lacks that are apparent in the total human makeup which indicate that we are far from using all the capabilities of this tremendous organ, the brain. In this connection Dr. Lauretta Bender, famous for her Bender-Gestalt test for visual motor perceptual problems, made significant comments at a learning disabilities conference at Napa, California, in November of 1969 regarding brain damage. Her observation was that everyone is brain damaged to some degree since one would not expect to find a perfect brain.

The essential difference between most of us who function successfully is our ability to compensate in one way or another for the disfunctioning that we have. We become obsessive, compulsive, perseverative, or in cases of brilliance—physicists, statisticians, mathematicians, etc. Thus the terms to use are minimal brain dysfunction or minimal cerebral dysfunction, or some of the other appropriate diagnoses listed in Chapter 3 on page 23.

BIBLIOGRAPHY FOR CHAPTER EIGHT

Alvarez, Walter C., Enuresis, *Modern Medicine*, p. 95, June 16, 1969.

Ayres, A. Jean, Southern California Perceptual-Motor Tests Manual, Western Psychological Services, 1968.

Bender, Lauretta, Neuropsychiatric Disturbances, Part II, chap. 5, p. 45, *Dyslexia, Diagnosis and Treatment of Reading Disorders,* edited by **Keeney,** Arthur H., and **Keeney,** Virginia T., C. V. Mosby Company, St. Louis, 1968.

Bettman, Jerome W. Jr., **Stern,** Earl L., **Whitzell,** Leon J., and **Gofman,** Helen F., Dominance Has Little to Do with Dyslexia, Abstract, *Modern Medicine,* March 11, 1968, p. 117, Original Paper: Cerebral Dominance in Developmental Dyslexia, *Archives of Ophthalmology,* Vol. 78, pp. 722-729, 1967.

Boder, Elena, A Neuropediatric Approach to the Diagnosis and Management of School Behavior and Learning Disorders, *Learning Disorders,* Vol. II, p. 22, edited by **Helmuth,** Jerome, Special Child Publications, Seattle, 1966.

Clements, Sam D., Project Director, Minimal Brain Dysfunction National Project on Learning Disabilities in Children, *N & SDCP* Monograph, Phase 2, Section 5, Part 2, p. 55, Public Health Service Publication No. 2015, Superintendent of Documents, Government Printing Office, Washington, D.C., 1969.

Clements, Sam D., and **Peters,** John E., Minimal Brain Dysfunctions in the School-Age Child: Diagnosis and Treatment, *Archives of General Psychiatry,* Vol. 6, pp. 185-197, March, 1962.

Colodny, Dorothy, **Kenny,** Carolyn, and **Kurlander,** L. F., The Educationally Handicapped Child: The Physician's Place in a Program to Overcome Learning Disability, *California Medicine,* Vol. 109, No. 1, pp. 15-18, California Medical Association, July, 1968.

Cratty, Bryant J., and **Martin,** Margaret M., The Effects of a Program of Learning Games upon Selected Academic Abilities in Children with Learning Difficulties. Monograph, University of California, Los Angeles, September, 1970.

Eeg Olofsson, O., **Petersen,** I., **Sellden,** U., The Development of the Electroencephalogram in Normal Children from the Age of 1 through 15 years, Paroxysmal Activity, *Neuropadiatrie*—2—pp. 375-404, 1971. Dept. Clin. Neurophysiol, Univ. Goteborg. Abstract: *Epilepsy Abstracts,* Excerpta Medica, Vol. 4, No. 9, September, 1971.

Ertl, John P., Using Speed of Brain Waves to Test IQ, *Medical World News,* p. 26, March 8, 1968.

Farmer, Thomas W., *Pediatric Neurology,* Chapter 2, p. 76, Hoeber Medical Division, Harper & Row, 1964.

Fuisz, Robert E., **Fuisz,** Richard C., *The Hyperactive Child,* Meeting Street School Screening Test (MSSST), Neurological Exam, pp. 22-29, prepared for CIBA Pharmaceutical Company, Summit, N.J., by Medcom, Inc., 1971.

Gross, Mortimer D., and **Wilson,** William C., Behavior Disorders of Children with Cerebral Dysrhythmias: Successful Treatment of Subconvulsive Dysrhythmia with Anticonvulsants, *Archives of General Psychiatry,* Vol. II, p. 610, December, 1964.

Harris, Theodore L., **Otto,** Wayne, **Barrett,** Thomas C., and **Mattingly,** Jane, Summary and Review of Investigations Relating to Reading, July 1, 1966, to June 30, 1967, *The Journal of Educational Research,* Vol. 61, No. 6, p. 247, February, 1968.

Klinkerfuss, G. H., **Lange,** P. H., **Weinberg,** W. A., and **O'Leary,** J. L., Electroencephalographic Abnormalities of Children with Hyperkinetic Behavior, *Neurology,* Vol. 15, No. 10, pp. 883-891, 1965.

Kock, C., and **Melchior,** J. C., Headache in Childhood, a Five Year Material from a Pediatric University Clinic, Abstract from *Hemicrania,* Vol. I, No. 3, p. 11, *Journal of the Migraine Trust,* London 1969. Original Article, Dan. Med. Bull., 16/4 (109-114), 1969.

Kohen-Raz, Reuven, Ataxiametric Measurement of Static Balance, Abstract, Modern Medicine, May 3, 1971, p. 86. Original paper: Developmental Patterns of Static Balance Ability and Their Relation to Cognitive School Readiness, *Pediatrics,* Vol. 46, pp. 276-285, 1970.

Meier, John H., Prevalence and Characteristics of Learning Disabilities Found in Second Grade Children, *Journal of Learning Disabilities,* Vol. 4, No. 1, p. 10, January, 1971.

Oettinger, Leon Jr., **Nekonishi,** Harold, and **Gill,** Ian G., Cerebral Dysrhythmia Induced by Reading (Sub-Clinical Reading Epilepsy). *Develop. Med. Child Neurol.,* Vol. 9, pp. 191-201, 1967.

Paine, Richmond S., Organic Neurological Factors Related to Learning Disorders: Conventional Neurological Examination, chapter 1, pp. 8-9, *Learning Disorders,* Vol. 1, edited by **Hellmuth,** Jerome, Special Children Publications, Seattle, 1965.

Rabe, Edward F., Minimal Brain Dysfunction National Project on Learning Disabilities in Children, Phase 2, Appendix A—Neurological Evaluation, *N&SDCP* Monograph, pp. 69-71, Public Health Service Publication No. 2015, Superintendent of Documents, Government Printing Office, Washington, D.C., 1969.

Small, Joyce G., Abstract: Characteristics of EEG of Child Mentally Impaired, *Modern Medicine,* p. 156, June 16, 1969. Original Article: Epileptiform Electroencephalographic Abnormalities in Mentally Ill Children, *J. Nerv. Ment. Dis.,* 147: 341-348, 1968.

Small, Joyce, G., The Organic Dimension of Crime, *Archives of General Psychiatry,* Vol. 15, pp. 82-89, July, 1966.

Stevens, Janice R., **Sachdev,** Kuldip, and **Milstein,** Victor, Behavior Disorders of Childhood and the Electroencephalogram, *Archives of Neurology,* Vol. 18, pp. 160-177, February, 1968.

Torres, F., and **Ayres,** F. W., Evaluation of the Electroencephalogram of Dyslexic Children, *EEG and Clinical Neurology,* 24: 286, 1968.

Wender, Paul H., foreword by **Eisenberg,** Leon, *Minimal Brain Dysfunction in Children,* pp. ix, x, Wiley-Interscience, a Division of John Wiley & Sons, Inc., New York, 1971.

Whitsell, Leon Jr., Learning Disorders as a School Health Program: Neurological and Psychiatric Aspects, *California Medicine,* Vol. III, No. 6, p. 433, December, 1969.

Williams, Denis, Abstract: Habitual Criminal Is Likely to Have an Abnormal EEG, *Modern Medicine,* p. 11, July 27, 1970. Original article: Neural Factors Related to Habitual Aggression, *Brain,* 92: 503-520, 1969.

CHAPTER NINE

THE USE AND MISUSE OF TESTING

A good battery of tests sparks the activity of special educational committees and programs of most schools. But like any "battery," it has its positives and negatives. So do not be misled.

The main purpose in testing a pupil with a learning disability in the ordinary school situation is to identify the area(s) of strength as well as the specific area(s) of disability for which there are the means of remediation. Appropriate retesting is carried out to determine the degree of correction and to find out if it has been partial or complete. A sequence of tests performed annually serves as a gauge on the pupil's progress in a special program.

Academic progress should definitely not be the sole measuring device, as this story about Nancy will illustrate. At nine years of age, the girl was virtually a non-reader. She was shy and withdrawn with a poor self-image in addition to the usual neurological impairment. The emotional climate at home was bad—quite inadequate for Nancy's progress in school.

The girl spent two years in her school's "Educationally Handicapped Program" but made very little progress in reading. She would have been discharged from the program but her special teacher reported that it had taken Nancy two years to build up sufficient self-confidence and self-image to take on reading. Therefore she was kept in the program and gradually made the desired progress.

What other purposes can be served by testing?

In centers of higher learning, where much research is being carried out, it is necessary to test beyond the point for which corrective measures are available. The extended testing is designed to develop the diagnostic clarification which is a good basis for creating a therapeutic program. After tests are developed that can accurately pinpoint the problem area, then the means of correcting the problem can be more precisely administered. A problem is always best solved when the cause is identified and appropriate corrective measures can be applied. These may hold it in check or allow for adjustments that compensate and bring about the desired result.

Even if the cause is unknown, an improper process can be detected and stopped in favor of more corrective measures. It is more reassuring to know the cause, but such knowledge is not always essential.

We do not know why some children see letters backward, but remedial steps can be taken to correct the troublesome characteristic. We do not know why some children are overactive, but we can prescribe adequate corrective measures to help them.

How can tests be measured?

Many people inside and outside of school are unaware of available tests for children with learning disabilities. Therefore, *no use is misuse*. A few are aware of the tests but can't be bothered. What a tragedy!

Parents can misuse tests. Mr. and Mrs. "Unconvinced," for example, had a boy with a pronounced learning disability. He also had the annoying behavior associated with it. His behavior problem was caused more by the parents' attitude and the way they carried on about their child's problem than by the learning problem.

The teacher, principal and school psychologist did their part in referring, testing and developing a program of specialized instruction to help the boy. The parents cooperated fully until informed of what needed to be done to help their boy. They simply refused to believe the extent of his trouble.

Instead of continuing their cooperation, they embarked on a long trek from one specialist to another to have their son tested. They searched in vain for someone to tell them their son was perfectly normal, without any problem at all. Such misuse of tests led to the rejection of reality by the parents, compounding the boy's basic learning problem many times over.

What is the possibility of false negatives in testing?

No news is not always good news. Take the case of Tom, for example. An underachiever in school work, he was given a battery of selected tests. The result: All work done within normal limits.

The conclusions of the tests were misleading. They provided a negative result, because the battery of tests used did not include all the areas of possible difficulties. Tom was given tests that covered visual acuity (Snellen eye chart), and visual-motor perception. But tests for auditory problems were not included. The tests that were conducted were good as far as they went. They simply did not go far enough so the trouble was not uncovered.

The audiometer test must be properly evaluated because it can be misleading in some cases even when the results are reported as being "normal." See chapter six, page 41 for further explanation.

What areas should be considered in the full spectrum of testing?

Five major areas in testing are Learning, Behavior, Physical, Neurological and Sociological.

Each area has sub-divisions—some with more, some with fewer. In certain sub-divisions there are tests that are "musts." They form a basic test battery as shown on page 78.

Is there flexibility in the Basic Test Battery?

The very fact that there are no two pupils alike presupposes flexibility in testing them. The testor's experience with the tests he is administering provides still another important variable. There are a variety of tests for the same area and in some cases for the same item to be tested. For example, the WISC is the IQ test preferred by many school psychologists but not every needy child can take the WISC. He might be too young, too immature, or possessed by too great an emotional problem. Thus the testor must use good judgment in substituting the IQ test best suited to the circumstances in the child under study.

Other IQ tests include the Goodenough, the Peabody Picture Vocabulary Test, the Stanford Binet and others.

The Weschler Intelligence Scale for Children (WISC) is preferred because it measures both Verbal and Performance abilities in 10 to 12 different sub-divisions. Pupils who are not learning at a level equal to their IQ and are thereby called "underachievers" show the following characteristics in the WISC:

1 There is a discrepancy between the verbal and performance scores—perhaps 10 to 15 more points difference between them (Rabinovitch 1968).

2 There is scatter in the Verbal and/or Performance sub test scores—some scores are low, some high, others in between (Neville 1966).

3 There may be both discrepancy and scatter. These three clinically observed features of the WISC in the learning disability child were not fully borne out in a study by Ackerman, Peters and Dykman (1971).

MAJOR AREA	TEST	MEASURES
Learning	Wechsler Intelligence Scale for Children (WISC)—suitable for 2nd graders or older. Otherwise, the Stanford Binet Test is used.	IQ
	Bender-Gestalt	Visual Motor Perception
	Wide Range Achievement Tests	Grade Level Achievement in each subject.
	—Reading	Oral word recognition only.
	—Spelling	Spelling
	—Arithmetic	Arithmetic
	Gates Reading Survey, Gray Oral or Gillmore Test	Reading comprehension
	Wepman Auditory Discrimination Test	Auditory discrimination
Behavior	Bender-Gestalt (provides both emotional and perceptual information)	Emotional profile
	Sentence completion	Emotional profile
	Draw a person	Emotional profile
	Burks' Behavior Rating Scale for Organic Brain Dysfunction	Vegetative Autonomic, Perceptual-Discriminative, Social-Emotional
Physical	Snellen with plus lenses	Visual acuity
	Telebinocular or Titmus	Visual acuity
	Audiometer	Sound acuity
Neurological	Neurological Examination, designed for learning problems (see Chapter 8)	Neurological impairment or dysfunction
Sociological	Interview of parent, preferably at home	Social situation at home

Other tests in the area of learning are:

The Frostig Developmental Test of Visual Perception.
This examination checks: (1) Visual-motor coordination, (2) Figure-ground perception, (3) Constancy of shape, (4) Position in space, and (5) Spatial relationships.

The application of the results of this test and the integration of visual perceptual techniques is described in the article by Dr. Frostig, "Visual Perception, Integrative Functions and Academic Learning" (1972).

The Illinois Test for Psycholinguistic Ability (ITPA).

Twelve areas of the learning process are tested in order to determine the specific area or areas of difficulty and of strength. Although the ITPA is mainly used by speech and hearing specialists it is also quite useful in other aspects of the learning disability spectrum. For example, a child may not have a speech or hearing problem as such. The audiometer test and the Wepman Auditory Discrimination test are within normal limits but the child is not learning. An ITPA is done only to reveal that the problem is due to poor auditory sequential memory and poor auditory closure. Perceptual remedial reading specialists would do well to have the ITPA available to use for the appropriate child to diagnose and to set up a specific program. The test takes about 2½ hours to administer and thus is not practical for use in a routine test battery. Like any test it takes time and experience to learn how to use it proficiently.

The top chronological age on the score sheet is ten years, but the test could also be used on older pupils whose learning level falls within the limits of the test. For instance, a fourteen year old in high school who is reading at a 4th grade level could be tested with the ITPA. Some of his scores may go over the ten-year limit but other scores may well denote the area(s) of his problem.

The areas of the ITPA are:

Auditory Reception
Visual Reception
Auditory Association
Visual Association   **Representational Level**
Verbal Expression
Manual Expression

Grammatic Closure
Visual Closure
Auditory Sequential Memory
Visual Sequential Memory   **Automatic Level**
Auditory Closure
Sound Blending

The important relationship between visual perception, visual memory, visual discrimination and visual sequential memory and the tests that measure them are given by Doctors Guthrie and Goldberg (1972).

Some speech therapists and speech pathologists are pleased by the results obtained because they are a guide in setting up a therapy program for those with an aphasia problem.

What can be learned by comparing silent and oral reading?

Some children pronounce words while reading or they silently say the words to themselves. These should be tested in silent and oral reading and their results should be compared. If the silent reading is poorer, then the child should read into a tape recorder. Afterward the child should listen to what was recorded while he looks at the actual words. This exercise reinforces the internal checking mechanism which is weak and for which the child was substituting an external mechanism. These can be referred to as internal or external auditing loops. The external loop functions each time we speak.

School psychologists are particularly trained in the behavior area. They have at their disposal tests that can give an adequate appraisal of the pupil's emotional profile. This can also include their observations of the pupil in the classroom, on the playground and during the testing and interviewing periods.

Obviously, some pupils have purely a learning problem and do not need psychological testing. A fair number of pupils will need varying amounts of such testing. A few pupils will need an in-depth study not only involving the school psychologist but also specific referral to a clinical psychologist or to a psychiatrist trained for the pediatric-age group.

An excellent discussion of "Early Prediction of Reading Disability" is given by de Hirsch and Jansky (1968). The authors compare numerous available tests as to their merits. The study is worth the effort by those who take testing seriously and who would avoid the subtle mistakes to which improper usage of testing can lead.

Further information about the evaluation of a child with a learning disability plus an extensive list of tests helpfully categorized with specific comments regarding intent of uses, has been done by Bateman and Schiefelbusch (1969).

BIBLIOGRAPHY FOR CHAPTER NINE

Ackerman, Peggy T., **Peters,** John E., and **Dykman,** Roscoe A., Children with Specific Learning Disabilities: WISC Profiles, *Journal of Learning Disabilities,* Vol. 4, No. 3, pp. 150-166, March, 1971.

Bateman, Barbara, D., and **Schiefelbusch,** Richard L., Educational Identification, Assessment, and Evaluation Procedures, Minimal Brain Dysfunction in Children, *N&SDCP* Monograph, Phase Two, of a three-phase project of the U.S. Department of Health, Education and Welfare, Public Health Service, Publication No. 2015, in Section II, pp. 5-16 and Appendix I, pp. 18-20, 1969.

de Hirsch, Katrina, and **Jansky,** Jeanette J., Early Prediction of Reading Disability, chapter 4, pp. 21-31, *Dyslexia, Diagnosis and Treatment of Reading Disorders,* edited by **Keeney,** Arthur H., and **Keeney,** Virginia T., C.V. Mosby Co., St. Louis, 1968.

Frostig, Marianne, Visual Perception, Integrative Functions and Academic Learning, *Journal of Learning Disabilities,* Vol. 5, No. 1, pp. 1-15, January, 1972.

Guthrie, John T., and **Goldberg,** Herman K., Visual Sequential Memory in Reading Disability, *Journal of Learning Disabilities,* Vol. 5, No. 1, pp. 41-46, January, 1972.

Neville, Donald, The Intellectual Characteristics of Severely Retarded Readers and Implications for Teaching Techniques, *Learning Disorders,* Vol. 2, pp. 285-287, Special Child Publications, Seattle, 1966.

Rabinovitch, R. D., Reading Problems in Children: Definitions and Classifications, chapter 1, p. 2, *Dyslexia, Diagnosis and Treatment of Reading Disorders,* edited by **Keeney,** Arthur H., and **Keeney,** Virginia T., C. V. Mosby Company, St. Louis, 1968.

CHAPTER TEN

THE CONVINCING WITNESS OF HANDWRITING

What are the four most common methods of communicating?

Hearing, speaking, reading and writing is our communications quartet. Ask a simple question and you receive a simple answer.

But, consider for a moment the unfortunates who are unable to perform adequately any one or any combination of those complex functions of communication and suddenly the answers do not seem so simple.

Writing, like speaking, is the final result of a complicated series of functions. The hand and fingers of a writer do not put down random scrawls. They respond to messages from the brain and print or write out information stored in the memory banks of the various sensory areas of the human computer. Or they may write down, by the process of copying, that which the eyes behold at the moment.

What Is Dysgraphia?

Dorland's Illustrated Medical Dictionary, 24th edition, describes dysgraphia as "the inability to write properly because of ataxis, tremor or motor neurosis." But even when there are no motor coordinating difficulties, faulty visual perception can cause poor writing. Just as the speech mechanism cannot produce a sound properly if the hearing mechanism does not hear it correctly, the writing mechanism cannot accurately duplicate what the seeing mechanism does not see correctly.

"Speech mechanism" involves speech areas of the brain from which nerves leave to control various organs of speech—mouth, tongue, throat, nose, lungs, etc.

The "hearing mechanism" is the ear, with the hearing portion of the brain and its connecting nerves.

The "seeing mechanism" involves the eyes, the seeing portion of the brain and its connecting nerve pathways.

The "writing mechanism" involves that motor area of the brain and the connecting nerves that flow from it to the hand and arm.

When an undistorted image is picked up by the eye and sent to the seeing portion of the brain and is there distorted through improper visual perception, this distorted image will then be reproduced in this improper fashion by the hand. Or, if a distorted visual image is stored in a visual memory area, the hand will reproduce it later in its perceptually distorted form, even though the brain's motor mechanism for fine coordination is functioning properly.

Visual acuity difficulties can cause writing distortions. A person with a certain degree of astigmatism can look at a perfectly round circle and draw it as an oval. An eyeball with astigmatism picks up the image of the circle on the retinal area which is shaped in an oval fashion like a spoon instead of a uniform sphere. Proper glasses are needed to correct this type of problem. But eyeglasses will not correct a visual perception problem.

What can be done for a dysgraphic poor reader?

If a pupil's hearing and auditory functions are within normal limits, or are less impaired than the reading and visual functions, then they should be taught by auditory means. Teaching material should be put on tape so the student can listen to it.

This is being done by special education teachers in some schools. Results are quite rewarding.

While using additional methods of getting information to the pupil through properly functioning sensory systems, the teacher should also keep up the remedial training of the impaired systems.

Working through strengths to aid and correct weaknesses is a basic principle of life—the more so among those with learning disabilities.

Response to medication falls into two basic categories:

1 The improvement in writing, as noticed in a few days.

2 The improvement in writing over a few weeks or months.

In both cases there is a reversion to the previous style of writing when medication is stopped during the earlier phases of treatment. The more the brain is able to correct itself with the assistance of medication by developing an improved habit pattern the less the degree of reversion when medication is stopped.

Does medication assist the functioning, coordinative, or perceptual aspect of writing?

Where and how medicine acts is difficult to determine, but the fact that it does act is obvious.

This good effect of properly applied and controlled medication serves as a vivid example of the way medication can be most helpful in assisting the brain to receive information and to use it in daily expression in a more appropriate fashion.

Most of the time it is the working together of medication plus specific training that is essential for correcting as much as possible these learning disabilities. Special training for the dysgraphic pupil includes various fine motor coordination techniques—especially those involving the fingers, hands and arms and visual perceptual motor procedures.

What if these methods don't help the dysgraphic person?

Not all dysgraphic people can be helped by medication. To keep them from falling behind in school while effective treatment is being sought, the instructor should permit them to do one or both of the following:

1   Turn in oral responses to tests, instead of written ones.

2   Use the typewriter. Extra care should be taken to allow them to learn to type *at their speed*. Often they cannot keep up with the usual pace of a typewriting class. The same coordination problem that kept them from developing skill in writing may also affect their typing. But the repetitious exercises in typing can help to improve fine coordination. What the typewriter prints can be read and this delights teacher and pupil alike.

Can medication help the dysgraphic person?

A picture is worth a thousand words, says the Chinese adage. It's true also for the analyst who tests dysgraphic people.

The following examples of drawings, printing and writing show what proper medication can do in a fairly good percentage of cases.

SECTION ONE

"PERFORMANCE FLUCTUATIONS WITHOUT MEDICATION"

These first two examples demonstrate performance fluctuations, that is, for no apparent reason there is a day-to-day change in the writing ability of a learning disabled child.

1st example

J.J. is a nine-year-old boy in fourth grade who shows moderate changes.

2nd example

D.M., also a fourth-grade boy, shows the following variations in handwriting and emotions. The first example illustrates fairly good work. On another day, D.M. cannot even begin to put his abilities to work.

SECTION TWO

"EXAMPLES OF HANDWRITING BEFORE AND AFTER MEDICATION"

3rd example

S.R. was a five-year-old girl in kindergarten. Her drawing ability improved with the use of dextroamphetamine sulphate (Dexedrine®).

4th example

Len, age 12, was in an EH class for fourth, fifth and sixth graders. His medications were methylphenidate (Ritalin®) and trifluoperazine (Stelazine®).

5th example

Danny, age 12, was in sixth grade but spent more time with the principal than with the teacher due to a severe class disruptive behavior. His medication, amphetamine tannate (Obotan®), brought an *immediate* change in handwriting as well as in classroom behavior. He is one of the "miracle" cases. Any day his medicine was forgotten brought immediate and complete regression in both handwriting and behavior.

6th example

Regina, aged six, was in first grade. Her medication was dextroamphetamine sulphate (Dexedrine®). In contrast to Danny (example 5), her medication brought about a *gradual* change over four months.

7th example

R.E. was a boy almost 10 years old in fourth grade. His behavior was good and he was not hyperactive but amphetamine tannate (Obotan®) altered his printing ability.

8th example

Ronnie was six years old in kindergarten. He was one of the rare cases of mirror printing being corrected by Ritalin® alone without any perceptual training.

SECTION THREE

"HANDWRITING CHANGES RESULTING FROM DIFFERENT MEDICATIONS AND THEIR COMBINATIONS."

9th example

B.K. was an eight-and-a-half-year-old boy in third grade. His work samples demonstrate the effects obtained by one medication as compared with two medications, thioridazine (Mellaril ®) and ethosuximide (Zarontin ®).

10th example

L.D., was a six-and-a-half-year-old girl in second grade.

11th example

Ronald for 17 months has been on two medications:
Ritalin® and Stelazine®. Ritalin® subsequently lost its effectiveness and was replaced by Obotan®. It, along with Stelazine®, regained the previous good results.

Example 1-1 • Poor printing one day (*no medication involved*).

The seeds we'h planted in the
grew into large plants.

When we sming we give chid
rubber water wing to wear

If it is the teachers desk
there in the corner.

Father fixed the book
with some sand paper and

2. The seeds we planted in the eart
grew into large plants.

3. When we swim we give child
rubber wings to wear.

4. That's the teacher's desk over three
the corner.

5 Father fixed the bookshelf with s
sandpaper and paint.

Example 1-2 • Good writing another day *(no medication involved)*.

"Pretty, prett
I heard a sr
calling.
I looked a bo
side
And saw that
The sky was
was green.
The sunlight
Falling
On woods an
d andendelio
Which sho

Example 2-1 • Good work one day (medication not involved).

Example 2-2 • Poor work on another day *(medication not involved)*.

Example 3-1 • Before medication.

Example 3-2 • On Dexedrine®.

men

afraid of the white

landed

swinging

on.

distad

screamed

strat   3.   spring

squirrel   3.

three   ill

Example 4-1 • Before medication.

A wave.
Skipped from one rock to
We didn't want cassidy
He was not afraid of loeing his ow

stones.
racing.
helped
parents
fell
into
roar
earlier
Meatt
After

new
quick
school

firemen
twice
2nd

Example 4-2 • After use of Ritalin® and Stelazine®

helping c

thanking c
canhnl?
eat c
see c
look c
seeing c
leslie c
heting c ?
asking c
learning c ?

Example 5-1 • Without medication.

Language p.9,52

1. The river tumbled down t...
2. Tony sold goobers to all the ...
3. The good cooks fried cornmea...
4. The river overflowed its ban...
5. The villagers shucked the goo...
6. They threw the kernels into ...
7. The lumberjacks emptied the ...
8. They dumped salt and some ...
9. The whole mess boiled und...
10. The steam filled the air ...
11. The people scrambled ...
12. Tony saved the town. ☺

The

End

Example 5-2 • Results from one day on Obotan®.

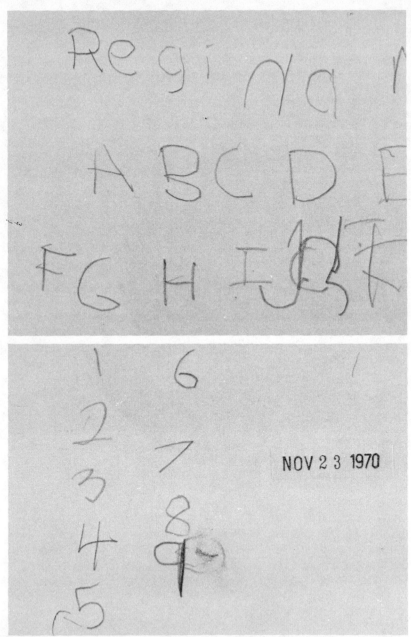

Example 6-1 • Without medication.

A B C D E F G H J K

1 2 3 4 5 6 7 8 9

R e g i n g

1 2 3 4 5 6 7 8 9 10

A B C D E F G H I

Example 6-2 • After two and four months of Dexedrine®.

1 2 3 4 5 6

A a   B d   C c   D b   E e   F f

1 2 3 4 5 6 7 8 9 10
A a B b C c D d E E F f G g H h I i
L i   Kk L I M m   N n O o P P
Q q R r S s T t

1 2 3 4 5 6 7 8 9 10

A a B b C c D d E E F f G g

Example 7-1 • On Obotan®.
Example 7-2 • Off Obotan®.
Example 7-3 • Back on Obotan®.

Ronnie was six years old in kindergarten. He was one of the rare cases of mirror printing being corrected by drug alone without any perceptual training.

JUL 1 0 1969

Example 8-1 • Before medication.

AUG 5   1969

RONNIE

Example 8-2 • After use of Ritalin®.

Example 9-1 • Spelling with Mellaril® alone.

Spelling test after three days off Zarontin. I have underlined the spelling words; he knew them perfectly after three days home study, then he blew the test.

need to clean the boat. With soap and
it.

— Excellent! spelling test
Bruce!

hot air dried the rain from her hair

trail just mist a pair of goat's head
missed

ch year Mother sends them a creampie

Spelling test one week later, after putting him back

on Zarontin for one week at one a day. And the

words were more difficult than the previous week.

Example 9-2 • Spelling with Mellaril® plus Zarontin®.

Example 10-1 • Printing without medication.

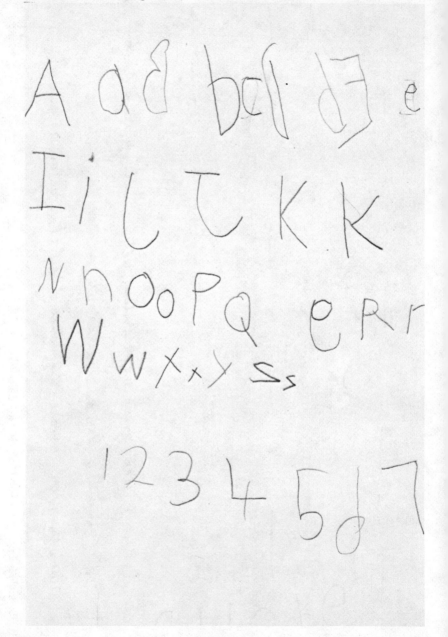

Example 10-2 • Printing with Ritalin® alone.

DEC 1

A B C D e F G H I J
R S T U V W X Y Z

1 2 3 4 5 6 7

A B c D e F g H i J K

1 2 3 4 5 6 7 8 9 10

L a u n i e

Example 10-3 • Printing with Ritalin® and Stelazine®.

Ronald for 17 months has been on two medications: Ritalin® and Stelazine®. Ritalin® subsequently lost its effectiveness and was replaced by Obotan®. It, along with Stelazine®, regained the previous good results.

Example 11-1 • All Ronald accomplished in one-and-a-half hours because medication lost effectiveness.

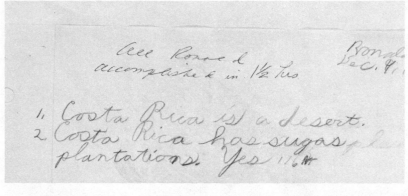

Example 11-2 • This math was all Ronald could produce in 50 minutes.

Ronald did th
paper in 30 minutes.

Ronald

1. That is a special class.

2. He is a very grouchy man.

3. They are sitting on the moss.

4. His father explained that he w

5. When your leg herts you limp.

6. He is a lame man.

7. Sheep dog's are shaggy dog's.

8. Some people have brown eyebr

9. You are very polite ▮▮▮ today

10. I like to drink tea with sug

11. The cars started down the race

12. He gave a grunt and went.

13. There are birch trees in the forest

11-3

Example 11-3 • Regained ability from Obotan® and Stelazine® enabled Ronald to write 22 lines in only 30 minutes.

THE ROLE OF MEDICINE

Since many people have been emotionally prejudiced against the use of medicine for children with learning problems this chapter must be read with the utmost objectivity. It is imperative that the uninitiated understand that this information is offered with conviction based on fact that proper and positive use of medication can indeed help children with learning disabilities. When they see the good results, adults respond enthusiastically—sometimes dramatically—as mixed-up lives are salvaged, educational failure turned to success, and troubled homes made peaceful again.

Without medicine, hundreds of children would go on to develop varying degrees of the "failure syndrome" which has become a major cause of ego destruction. This unfortunate turn of events leads many to become psychotics, neurotics, addicts, alcoholics and chronic welfare recipients.

The thinking of many has been prejudiced against the use of medicine in treating learning disabilities by the following excesses:

1   The epidemic *misuse* of drugs and dope has set all our emotions on edge, and that is understandable. But! what about the proper diagnostic and medically controlled use of medicines which have proven their effectiveness?

2   Unfortunately, the sensationalism of the news media is all too often built on negativism. Therefore when medicine *properly used* brings about a *sensational, positive result* the press can see it only in terms of the first point above. Earnest people are understandably troubled by such headlines as, "Pep Pills Prescribed for Learning Problems." Remember, there are two sides to most issues, and the negative is only one of them. Recently positive TV presentations have been encouraging. Let us hope that more will follow, both on TV and in the press.

This chapter seeks to introduce both sides concerning the reactions of specific medicines. Be informed! Read as a mature person and get the facts so you will be better able to discern between truth and error, right and wrong.

3   The administering of medicine is the treatment with a substance or chemical that is foreign to the human body and therefore may seem to the uninitiated as being unnatural and wrong. People who stress nutrition feel exceptionally strong on this point. Granted, proper nutrition is most essential for good physical health. All aspects of nutrition today should be evaluated through scientific research so that more people will include in their diets the necessary ingredients for growth (this includes the all-important interuterine growth period from one cell at conception to a newborn baby with billions of cells), development, maintenance, repair and general overall health. *Has everyone really achieved full, normal growth from his childhood nutrition?* The author is of the opinion that not everyone has. Or if they had proper nutrition, they were unable to assimilate or to utilize adequately the nutrients they received because of genetic and other reasons. The result: A central nervous system that misfunctions or dysfunctions because of a biochemical lack. Often this biochemical inadequacy can be made up by a chemical (medicine) that is administered deliberately to cause a helpful reaction with the electro-biochemical-enzymatic-hormonal mechanism of the nervous system and thus brings about varying degrees of proper function.

Proper medication under adequate control with minimal or no side effects has a high percentage of good response. Children whose nervous systems had been programmed for failure have been rescued by proper medical means. Thus the other necessary remedial education, exercise, perceptual testing and psychological measures could be more effective, leading eventually to a maximum overcoming of failure.

Don't let negative emotions or misinformation distort your perspective at this point. To see the dramatic recoveries through medicine is to experience intense joy. Imagine the gratification to all concerned when a child is snatched from failure and disgrace and put on the road to success through the simple prescription of a thoroughly tested medicine!

Basic principles and clinical information in abundance are considered next in this continuing discussion of the proper use of medicines in treating children with learning disabilities.

How effective is medication?

Good results are recorded in approximately 80 to 84 per cent of all cases treated; fair results are charted in 16 to 18 per cent of the cases; finally, from two to four per cent of all cases are not helped by medicines presently available. These percentages are taken from the author's records of private practice. A local school district had similar findings, recording 80 per cent on the side of good results from medicine.

As stated in chapter two, Dr. Wender (1971) in his book *Minimal Brain Dysfunction in Children* says there is a 50 to 70 per cent chance of good response and five to 10 per cent chance of the symptoms becoming worse.

Is medication used only for hyperkinetics?

Proper medication does more than glue a troublemaker to his seat so he won't "bug" the teacher (Clements 1969, and Gustafson and Coursin 1968). Amphetamine therapy was first demonstrated by Dr. Bradley in 1937 to show its ability to reduce hyperactivity (Bradley 1937). Dextroamphetamine sulfate (Dexedrine®) and methylphenidate hydrochloride (Ritalin®), for example, also help the learning process indirectly by increasing the attention span and concentration. In addition, they aid the memory and assist the patient to follow through on assignments. They also have a direct effect on the learning process, as pointed out by many specialists (Conners, Rothschild, Eisenberg, Schwartz and Robinson 1969, Conners 1970, Conners, Eisenberg, and Barcai 1967, Conners 1971, Conrad, Dworkin, Shai and Tobiessen 1971, and Solomons 1971).

Medicine can also:

... Aid the subtle hyperkinetic child (see discussion on this subject in chapter three, page 17)

... Reduce distractibility and fidgetiness

... Improve fine and gross coordination

... Decrease or eliminate stuttering or cluttering

... Improve pronunciation

... Reduce or eliminate temper or "acting out" behavior

... Reduce feelings of inadequacy, insecurity and inferiority

... Decrease mood swings

... Decrease or eliminate headaches or stomach aches

, ... Correct or reduce the problem of enuresis (bed wetting)

... Eliminate or improve such sleep problems as getting to sleep, restless sleep, nightmares, sleep walking, awakening tired or grouchy.

**Won't youngsters "grow out" of their
trouble without medication?**

No doubt a certain percentage of children with learning disabilities would outgrow their overactivity problem in a few years. But what about the educational, behavioral and emotional damage produced in the process? Dr. Wender (1971) states that failure to use medication gives the child a small chance of experiencing improvement. Many adults today who were hyperactive as children still suffer from the malady. In some it is quite obvious; others have learned to control it and build a facade of respectability. But inquiry brings their hyperactivity to the surface. With it are the physical, emotional, social, intellectual and spiritual problems it continues to generate. (See chapter eighteen, page 201, regarding the Adult Hyperkinetic Syndrome.)

**Can different medicines be used for learning problems
with or without a behavior problem?**

Definitely! Four categories of medicines are available. Their names denote their primary purposes. However, the category titles of anti-convulsants and stimulants are misnomers and do not correspond to their desired actions when used for these types of learning problems (Millichap 1968).

1 *Anti-Convulsants.* Aside from their obvious usage, this prescription is often beneficial as well to a patient with a learning problem who has never suffered from convulsions or had a family history of the same. Diphenylhydantoin (Dilantin®), primidone (Mysoline®), phensuximide (Milontin®), ethosuximide (Zarontin®)—these are examples of this type.

2 *Tranquilizers.* Many are on the market but only a few effectively treat our problem. Two of these are thioridazine hydrochloride (Mellaril®) and trifluopherazine (Stelazine®). Both belong to the phenothiazine chemical group of tranquilizers. A report in Science (Rappaport, Silverman, Hopkins and Hall 1971) indicates their effect on the auditory signal. The author has had a couple of cases of auditory agnosia helped by a phenothiazine. The usual side effect of a tranquilizer is drowsiness, but it is *never* the intent to make the patient drowsy. The effect can be regulated by adjusting the dosage or switching to another brand. Only rarely does a tranquilizer produce a reverse reaction and stimulate the patient.

3 *Stimulants.* This is the red flag to skeptics on medicine. Will you too react with your emotions rather than seeking to learn the truth? Most parents and patients who are overactive, high strung or quite

nervous react with wonder when stimulants for hyperkinetics are prescribed. Nevertheless, clinical experience shows that a high percentage of overactive patients react to stimulants with opposite effects. These stimulants produce paradoxically a reverse reaction which actually calms down the overactive patient so he can function normally.

Stimulants are divided into two basic chemical groupings.

a. The amphetamines—different chemical salts with such names as dextroamphetamine sulphate (Dexedrine®), amphetamine tannate (Obotan®), methamphetamine (Desoxyn®) and others. Differing clinical responses can be obtained even from these different salts or sub-groups. B. S. Rosner (1970) points out the effective influence of amphetamine on the learning behavior of animals following brain injury.

b. Methylphenidate hydrochloride (Ritalin®)—a medicine with no sub-groups at present (Martin 1967, and Nichamin and Barahal 1968).

4 *Psychic energizers.* Like tranquilizers, these can also be used for purely emotional problems. There are several kinds that can be administered. A few are effective in neurological problems, such as nortriptyline (Aventyl®) and imipramine (Tofranil®). A study in Vermont favored Tofranil for the treatment of hyperkinetic children (Huessy and Wright 1969). These two drugs also have a fairly high effectiveness in the treatment of Enuresis (bed wetting).

Does puberty alter the "reverse action" of stimulant medication?

Reverse action from drugs can occur in nearly all age groups, including puberty, adolescence and adulthood. Just because a patient reaches puberty or teen years is not cause enough to stop his taking of medication if the drug is producing proper benefits.

Are these medicines drugs?

All medicines are drugs and all drugs, by dictionary definition, are medicines. Dorland's Illustrated Medical Dictionary (24th edition) gives this definition:

Drug: Any chemical compound or any non-infectious biological substance, not used for its mechanical properties, which may be administered to or used on or for patients, either human or animal, as an aid in the diagnosis, treatment or prevention of disease or other abnormal condition, for the relief of pain or suffering, or to control or improve any physiological or pathological condition.

However, there is a vernacular or "street" definition for "drugs" which causes us to state that all drugs are not medicine.

For example, heroin, LSD, and marijuana—to name a few—are not medicines but they are drugs. Medical science as yet has not found a proper use for them.

Research is continuing to investigate LSD and marijuana but as yet the why, when and how of their proper use is not known.

Are these prescribed medicines "dope"?

Any medicine that can be habit forming or cause addiction in a person can *become* dope. Drugs like heroin, LSD, marijuana and the like are "dope" because there is no presently known effective and safe medical use for them. These drugs are illegal because they harm and destroy the body, soul and spirit of human beings.

Medicines used correctly help the whole person—body, soul and spirit. Dope is "ill-eagle" because when used by ill humans the result is "for the birds!"

Are not all stimulants labeled "dope"?

When he prescribes stimulant medicines, the specialist is looking for a calming effect that is a "reverse effect"—in 60 to 80 per cent of patients with neurologically involved learning disability. This effect is called a "neurological low," as contrasted with the "psychological high" that the addict and the experimenter seek from stimulants or "pep pills."

Here is the punch line (read it carefully):

It is virtually impossible for a properly diagnosed neurological hyper-kinetic patient to become addicted to a stimulant medication *either now or in the future* when the medicine gives the desired neurological *low* and not the psychological *high*. This fact has been observed for many years by several of us in the field. A study by Maurice W. Laufer (1971) would indicate that the proper use and response of these stimulants and other medications under adequate medical supervision and follow-up in childhood decreased the rate of not only addiction but also that of psychoses, neuroses and alcoholism in adolescent and adult life. This study did not support dire predictions, made by some, as to the outcome of long-term use of medications for hyperkinetic children.

Another discussion regarding the future variations that are possible in adulthood of these children with learning disabilities is presented by Dr. Wender (1971) in his chapter, "Prognosis of the MBD Syndrome."

Observe these further contrasts:

	Medical Workup	Source of medicine or drug	Those assisting in control and follow-up	Dosage	Results
Learning Disability	Yes	Physician Pharmacist Pharmaceutical Company	Parents Teacher Principal School Nurse	Regulated by physician	80% possibility good results
Experimenter Addict—doper	No	Dope pusher Kitchen sink Pseudo chemist	No one	Anything goes	Bum trip Brain damage Addiction Mental illness Death from OD (overdose) or from freaking out

Use a drug properly and it is a *good medicine.*
BUT misuse a drug, even a good one, *and it is DOPE.*

What is the true meaning of "addiction"?

The true meaning of the word involves (1) Physical dependence, (2) Psychological dependence, (3) Tolerance, and (4) Withdrawal.

The first means that the addict has developed a specific physical need for a drug to the point where actual cells of the body have so adjusted to the drug that the body cannot function adequately without it. The user is not really well off with the drug but has so adjusted to it, and therefore dependent upon it, that he is worse off without it.

Psychological dependence means that the user develops certain psychological symptoms which make him feel good, relaxed or carefree.

Tolerance means that in order to maintain and keep the desired effect of the drug more and more of it has to be taken because the body builds up resistance to it. Heavier doses are required to produce the desired results.

Finally, withdrawal refers to the period when a person no longer takes a given drug, inviting undesirable symptoms.

To become an "addict" or to become addicted to any given drug or medication, these four points should be realized, except in addicts who are addicted to amphetamines and marijuana. In these last-named cases there is only psychological dependence and no physical dependence is involved.

What is the main cause of addiction?

Emotional problems are the main scourge of drug addicts. These stem from problems in the home, inadequate academic achievement at school, etc.

Over a period of years the author has worked with addicts at a state institution. Although most of them came from inadequate home environments (two-thirds from broken homes), it was quite striking to observe that many addicts also had definite learning problems. They were underachieving with respect to their IQ level. This added frustration further "put down" such an individual and intensified his desire to escape reality through dope.

Stories told by these addicts about their learning and behavioral problems in school parallel many of those related by underachieving school children treated by the author in schools and in private practice. Dr. Tarnopol (1970) gives a good discussion on the correlation between delinquency and school failure as they relate to minimal brain dysfunction. Only God knows how many addicts could have been delivered from their fate if they had received the special educational help available today—*including* the assistance of proper medication! Educational-psychological therapy was used to improve the reading and intellectual abilities and thus the delinquent behavior of ten girls (Rice 1970).

Peer pressure to conform to the group, experimentation, and pleasure seeking also rate as strong influences that start people down the purposeless road of addiction.

Perhaps the following will help you to think about what makes something good or bad, including medicine.

Is water poisonous?

Yes. Water can kill. Excessive intake of the necessary liquid (five to ten gallons instead of the normal one-gallon dosage including water in food) is indeed poisonous. Excessive amounts of water in the cells of the body can result in water intoxication. This causes muscle tremors, cerebral (brain) edema and convulsions. Red blood cells hemolyze and thus break apart (Goodman and Gilman 1956). Oxygen, like water, is essential for life but it can damage or destroy certain parts of the brain if taken in high concentrations for too long a period (Goodman and Gilman 1965).

What determines bad use and good use?

God built into each human being a will which guides the individual in making choices. The right way often involves control outside oneself. That is why *in the case of medicine the proper use is under the care of a physician.* A car, a hand, or a pencil—each is helpful and good but each has killed when misused! It's the same with medicine. Can you name a good thing that has not been misused?*

How long should medication continue?

It is virtually impossible to predict in any one case how long the prescription should be extended. When Diabetes is discovered, for example, the patient understands that medication will be administered for the rest of his life. It becomes a life-and-death matter. But neurological problems are not as profound. They bear on a person's enjoyment of life but do not necessarily keep him alive.

Naturally, in the case of any problem the more quickly it is recognized and treated the better the chance for permanent correction and the end of medication. Large numbers of children on drugs no longer require them beyond the mid-point of their teen years. Once the patient realizes the satisfactory results of medication this acknowledgement itself makes the medicine acceptable for either short or long periods of time. Teenagers on medication want to get off it as quickly as possible. This is pretty good evidence that stimulants work paradoxically. They are not addictive.

How many medications need to be tried?

The duration of treatment depends upon each patient's response to it. Individualism is the key word. Approximately one-third to one-half of all patients enjoy satisfactory results from medication with the first or second choice. The remainder require further adjustments in the types and dosages before the correct one or the correct combination of medicine is determined.

There are some cases in which medication loses its effectiveness. If this occurs, a change is needed.

---

*The use of the "Interbang" is relatively new to the English language. Introduced in 1971, it accommodates the rhetorical question, and is thus used here. It is simply a combination of the exclamation point and the question mark. The Interbang is the first new punctuation mark for English since the quotation marks were introduced 300 years ago.

If one prescription doesn't work, will others fail too?

There are four categories of available medicines with several kinds in each category. That's a large selection from which to draw. Therefore it is *not true* that if one medicine or a one-medicine category does not work none of the others will either.

Occasionally it is necessary to make a clinical trial of a dozen or more different medications before the satisfactory result is obtained. Eighty per cent of all patients respond well largely because of the fact that there are between 15 and 20 medications from which to choose.

Can unpleasant side effects develop?

Any medication requiring a physician's prescription can at times produce undesirable side effects. Even some non-prescription items can do the same in certain types of individuals. Penicillin and aspirin are the usual culprits. They have a greater incidence of side effects—even dangerous ones—than the medicines we prescribe for learning disabilities. Side effects cease when the dosage is either reduced or discontinued. Side effects going on to permanent residual damage is essentially unknown.

What are some common side effects?

Amphetamines and Ritalin® can stimulate. When they do they are stopped immediately. Parents of patients should be informed about the possibility and are told what to do if it occurs. Insomnia, headache, stomach ache and decreased appetite are possible side effects in this kind of treatment.

Basic Principle

An individual's response to medication will never be discovered until he actually takes it into his system. No method has been worked out to predict reaction ahead of the administering. A physician makes the best choice he can, based upon his patient's history, the examination, test data and the totality of his clinical experience and judgment. Clinical follow-up then proceeds to observe results followed by appropriate adjustments in dosage or changes to other medication.

Drowsiness is the most common side effect of tranquilizers. But not infrequently, a reverse effect—stimulation, agitation, or irritability—can occur. Skin rash, too, can result from tranquilizers.

Anti-convulsant medications cause side effects less frequently than the other categories, according to the author's experience. Nevertheless, adequate checks must be made on the production of white cells and other blood difficulties. Such occurrence is quite rare.

The most common side effects from psychic energizers are drowsiness, dizziness and dry mouth.

Should medications for underachievers be given only when they are in school?

The central nervous system, including the brain, is functioning and learning *all the time*. It is taking in sensory stimuli even when an individual is asleep.

Of course, the learning situation is most precise and enduring in school so difficulties are usually most obvious there. But in order to assist the nervous system to function properly and to develop a more appropriate habit pattern the control of medicine is required both in and out of school, over a weekend and during vacations. A patient doesn't remove a cast from a broken leg when the limb is motionless. The same applies in the treatment of patients with learning disabilities.

A fair number of children require less medication during vacation periods. Some demand the same dosage and some even require more. Here's why:

To the child threatened by normal school life where he is unable to be like his peers and is unable to attain good grades for self esteem, vacation provides a relief from the strain. Other children, although frustrated also by learning problems, are more comfortable with the regimented life of school hours than with the unstructured time of vacation. At home, sometimes, their anxiety grows because there is little or no program, no clocks, bells and teachers to tell them what, when and how to do things. These types tend to act out all the more or to withdraw increasingly during hours away from school. Appropriate dosage increase affords better internal control and they are better able to cope with the situation.

When medication is not given on a weekend a child's worst day in school might be on Monday, yet parents may see no difference at home with regard to problem behavior on the weekend.

How many medications can a child take at one time?

Most patients require a combination of two types of medication. A fair number take only one. A few require more than two.

Which type of adult tends to resist medical treatment for underachievers?

1 A parent, teacher, or other individual who has never had to work with such children. The Indians have an appropriate expression as we

consider such people: "Never criticize another until you have walked in his moccasins." Let us be tolerant.

2   The father of the household usually, but not always, resists the idea of medication because:

a. He has less contact with his child than the mother. Even when father is home from work mother more frequently assists the child with homework and with special problems.

b. He tends to assume the problem is his wife's fault because she is with the children most.

c. The male ego finds it harder to admit his child has a problem.

d. The ratio of learning problems is seven or eight males to one female. That, plus the high hereditary factor, causes the father to over-react subconsciously in defense of his own ego feelings. To acknowledge his son's problem is to admit his own. The weaker the ego and the lower the self esteem the harder it is to admit a problem exists which may have caused the poor self image in the first place. If this "shoe" fits you, please take heart! Similar methods of help can be applied to adults which offer about a 50 per cent possibility of help through medication and other appropriate remedial assistance.

3   The teacher, school administrator, or other educational specialist who is an up-tight hyperkinetic adult who sees himself in a hyperkinetic child. This individual reacts negatively and often takes out hostile feelings against the children rather than reacting with patience and under-standing and thus help the ailing student.

Most often the physician sees a favorable change in the attitude of parents after their child begins to show progress in his learning or im-provement in his behavior. Yet these same parents often are quite resis-tant and a bit uncooperative at first because of fear and anxiety about medicine and drugs. If mother and father are at least willing to administer medication on a trial basis it is worthwhile because the results can be most convincing . . . and most rewarding.

Can medication help adults with a history of underachieving?

Medication most certainly can help, and has helped, parents and adults who had learning problems in school. If they still want help as adults because they are frustrated, high strung, nervous, moody, filled with anger and are eager to eliminate these traits from their lives, they should seek proper medical management.

Approximately half of all adults treated enjoy good results from medication. Chapter eighteen gives some specific clinical information on some of these adult patients.

Can an underachiever's problem affect an entire family?

Without doubt. Take your pick of any family and bet on it because there can be just one sufferer in the ancestral tree to infect an entire family. Add to this the fact that the effects of medication can differ among family members and the problem is compounded.

Are teen attitudes different from younger and older patients?

For the most part, teenage patients look at matters differently from children and adults. The teen years are difficult at best. When additional problems compound adolescence the change from youngster to adult is more difficult. To protect his developing self image he tries to act and think as though there were no problems, even when they are obvious. This attitude makes the remedy most difficult. People do not accept help until they admit they have a problem.

A teenager may submit to testing, the results of which he may verbally deny in the face of strong evidence, and then refuse remedial help because that would be tantamount to an admission: "I do have a problem." This course of action is hard on an ego that is already weakened by failure to learn adequately and to keep up with peers.

Most teenagers, when given an honest, straightforward appraisal of a problem with the suggestion of help which is coupled with patience and understanding, will respond and take medication on a trial basis. Then when they see the benefits, resistance usually fades and the ego gets a good boost.

Why slow down the central nervous system of hyperkinetics?

Learning requires first of all accuracy and concentration, not speed. A student approaches study slowly, gradually building up speed with improved proficiency. A nervous system with a short attention span and poor concentration makes learning most difficult. The good results from proper slowdown through medication are gratifying to all concerned.

Is masking symptoms with medication undesirable?

Some physicians, psychiatrists and psychologists feel that it is. But if a symptom interferes with adequate functioning and medicine can remove or reduce that symptom and improve functioning, isn't that desirable?

On the other hand, a symptom should not be removed with medication when that symptom is needed by the patient so he can work out his problem with professional counseling assistance and so he can gain the necessary insight into the cause of it. Even in these cases some medicine may be necessary to reduce the severity of a symptom that otherwise would incapacitate the person and fool the professional specialist.

What else but good can come from correcting symptoms by improved brain function, or by "masking" such symptoms as a short attention span, poor concentration, easy distractibility, poor follow-through, poor retention, temper tantrums, stuttering—and many more?

"You want to put my child on Dilantin®? I thought you said he did not have epilepsy!"

Dilantin® has been used for more than three decades to treat seizures, or convulsions or epilepsy. Today some heart specialists are using it in some patients with an irregular heart beat, called a cardiac arrhythmia (Gibber, Schmidt and Kutt, 1968, Damato 1969). Many medicines traditionally used for one condition are finding important usage in the treatment of other diseases. Many children take Dilantin® for learning-behavioral problems who do not have epilepsy. Certain tranquilizers are quite helpful for the mentally ill, but today they are also used to help problems connected with learning in children whose mental health is quite good. Most of the medications used in learning disabilities have other uses as well.

Many mothers of hyperkinetic children dread each phone call when school is in session.

"What's he done now?" they murmur at each ring.

What glad news it is when the voice at the other end tells a distraught mother something positive. "We're mighty happy with the improved work and conduct of your boy since you took him to the doctor for medication," the educational specialist might say. He might continue: "We're all encouraged now. It wasn't too long ago when the outlook was anything but good. Thought you would like to hear the news. . . ."

What a boost for parents! For their boy it is a double "Wow!" He is experiencing success at last, very quickly forgetting about past failure.

Some loss of appetite is a fairly common side effect of amphetamines (like Dexedrine® and Obotan®) and of Ritalin® even when they have the desired calming effect.

Appetite suppression is no indicator that the medication is working properly. Numerous patients are calmed by these stimulants and the appetite remains keen. A good number who have that effect and are calmed also regain a normal appetite anywhere from a couple of weeks to three or four months. If the appetite loss and weight loss is too drastic, then the medication is changed.

Basic Principle

Individualization is the watchword in the application of medication because positive effects and side effects can vary a lot even with the same dosage in different patients with identical problems. The difference in response to the same medication is brought out in the article "Each to His Own Therapeutic Dosage?" Sjoqvist, Vesell, Williams, and Brodie 1970). This is further emphasized by Kumar, Stolerman and Steinberg (1970).

Basic Principle

Nearly everything in life involves risk. Medication is no exception. The proper professional and scientific use of it for good far outweighs the risk of serious side effects. The risk involved in riding in a car or in taking penicillin by prescription or in taking aspirin without one—these are much greater than medication for learning disabilities under medical supervision. You haven't abandoned the automobile because more than fifty thousand people are killed each year on the highways.

The U.S. Department of Health, Education and Welfare has published a report (Zigler 1971) which clearly sets forth the correct use of these medications—in particular the amphetamines and Ritalin®, in treating children with learning disabilities. The report should be read by all interested persons.

Is any good thing in life not misused?

Use it right, it brings delight
Use it bad and you've been had
Use it wrong and you're forlorn

By refusing to accept the proper use of medication to aid children in the all-important task of learning, remember that the burden rests heavily upon you to come up with a better or an equally-as-good solution for improving the function of the brain.

Keep in mind this formula:

Proper diagnosis and proper medication with appropriate beneficial response and adequate medical and parental supervision *almost never produces addiction!*

BIBLIOGRAPHY FOR CHAPTER ELEVEN

Bradley, C., The Behavior of Children Receiving Benzedrine, *American Journal of Psychiatry,* Vol. 94, pp. 577-585, 1937.

Clements, Sam D., Project Director, Minimal Brain Dysfunction National Project on Learning Disabilities in Children, *N&SDCP* Monograph, Public Health Service Publication, No. 2015, pp. 61-62, U.S. Department of Health, Education, and Welfare, Washington, D.C., 1969.

Conners, C. K., **Rothschild,** G., **Eisenberg,** L., **Schwartz,** L. S., and **Robinson,** E., Dextroamphetamine Sulfate in Children with Learning Disorders: Effects on Perception, Learning and Achievement, *Archives of General Psychiatry,* Vol. 21: pp. 182-190, 1969.

Conners, C. K., Psychopharmacologic Treatment of Children, *Clinical Handbook of Psychopharmacology,* edited by **Di Mascio,** A., and **Shader,** R., Science House, New York, pp. 281-287, 1970.

Conners, C. K., **Eisenberg,** L., and **Barcai,** A., Effects of Dextroamphetamine on Children, Studies on Subjects with Learning Disabilities and School Behavior Problems, *Archives of General Psychiatry,* Vol. 17, pp. 473-485, October, 1967.

Conners, C. K., Recent Drug Studies with Hyperkinetic Children, *Journal of Learning Disabilities,* Vol. 4, No. 9, November, 1971.

Conrad, W. G., **Dworkin,** E. S., **Shai,** A., and **Tobiessen,** J. E., Effects of Amphetamine Therapy and Prescriptive Tutoring on the Behavior and Achievement of Lower Class Hyperactive Children, *Journal of Learning Disabilities,* Vol. 4, No. 9, November, 1971.

Damato, A. N., Diphenylhydantoin: Pharmacologic and Clinical Use, *Progress in Cardiovascular Diseases,* 12:1, 1969.

Gibber, J. T., Jr., **Schmidt,** D. H., and **Kutt,** H., Relationship Between the Plasma Level of Diphenylhydantoin Sodium and its Cardiac Antiarrhythmic Effects, *Circulation,* 38:363, 1968.
(The author is indebted to Robert D. Conn, M.D., Associate Professor, Physician-in-Chief, Harborview Medical Center, Seattle, Washington, for the two references above.)

Goodman, Louis S. and **Gilman,** Alfred, *The Pharmacological Basis of Therapeutics,* Excess Hydration, p. 769, 2nd edition, The Macmillan Co., New York, 1956.

Goodman, Louis S. and **Gilman,** Alfred, *The Pharmacological Basic of Therapeutics:* Untoward Effects of Oxygen Inhalation: Retrolental Fibroplasia; Oxygen Poisoning, pp. 900-901, 3rd edition, Macmillan Co., Toronto, 1965.

Gustafson, Sarah R., and **Coursin,** David R., *The Pediatric Patient,* Chapter

3, Part II, pp. 143-144, published by J. B. Lippincott, for Hoffmann-la Roche Laboratories, Philadelphia, 1968.

Huessy, Hans R., and **Wright,** Alice L., Graded Imipramine Regimen Favored in Hyperkinetic Children, *Journal of the American Medical Association,* Vol. 208, No. 9, Medical News section p. 1613, June 2, 1969.

Journal of Learning Disabilities, the entire November 1971 issue is given over completely to the subject of the role of medication in the treatment of learning disabilities and related behavior disorders.

Kumar, R., **Stolerman,** I. P. and **Steinberg,** Hannah, Psychopharmacology, Individual Reactions to Drugs, *Annual Review of Psychology,* Vol. 21, p. 614, edited by Farnsworth, P. R., *Annual Reviews,* Palo Alto, California, 1970.

Laufer, Maurice W., Long Term Management and Some Follow-up Findings on the Use of Drugs with Minimal Cerebral Syndromes, *Journal of Learning Disabilities,* Vol. 4, No. 9, pp. 519-522, November, 1971.

Martin, Daniel M., Hyperkinetic Behavior Disorders in Children: Clinical Results with Methylphenidate Hydrochloride, *Western Medicine,* pp. 23-27, January, 1967.

Millichap, J. Gordon, Drugs in Management of Hyperkinetic and Perceptually Handicapped Children, *Journal of the American Medical Association,* Vol. 206, No. 7, pp. 1527-1530, November 11, 1968.

Nichamin, Samuel J. and **Barahal,** George D., Faulty Neurologic Integration with Perceptual Disorders in Children, an Abridged Treatment Approach; a Two-Dimensional Program of Methylphenidate and Psychologic Management, *Michigan Medicine,* Vol. 67, No. 17, pp. 1071-1075, September, 1968.

Rappaport, M., **Silverman,** J., **Hopkins,** H. K., **Hall,** K., Phenothiazine Effects on Auditory Signal Detection in Paranoid and Non-Paranoid Schizophrenics, *Science,* Vol. 174, No. 4010, pp. 723-725, November 12, 1971.

Rice, Ruth Dianne, Educo-Therapy: A New Approach to Delinquent Behavior, *Journal of Learning Disabilities,* Vol. 3, No. 1, pp. 18-23, January, 1970.

Rosner, Burton S., Brain Functions: Pharmacological Influences, *Annual Review of Psychology,* edited by Farnsworth, P.R., Vol. 21, pp. 576-577, Palo Alto, California, 1970.

Sjoqvist, Folke, **Vesell,** Elliot S., **Williams,** R. Tecwyn, and **Brodie,** Bernard, Each to His Own Therapeutic Dosage?, *Medical World News,* Vol. 11, No. 30, pp. 18-19, McGraw-Hill, New York, 1970.

Solomons, G., Guidelines on the Use and Medical Effects of Psychostimulant Drugs in Therapy, *Journal of Learning Disabilities,* Vol. 4, No. 9, pp. 470-475, November, 1971.

Tarnopol, Lester, Delinquency and Minimal Brain Dysfunction, *Journal of Learning Disabilities,* Vol. 3, No. 4, pp. 200-207, April, 1970.

Tarnopol, Lester, *Learning Disorders in Children, Diagnosis, Medication, Education,* Little, Brown and Company, Boston, 1971.

Wender, Paul H., Management of the MBD Syndrome, The Decision to Treat with Medication: the Payoff Matrix, *Minimal Brain Dysfunction in Children,* chapter 5, p. 127, Wiley-Interscience, a Division of John Wiley & Sons, Inc., New York, London, Sydney, Toronto, 1971.
Ibid., Prognosis of the MBD Syndrome, chapter 4, pp. 75-85.

Zigler, Edward, Report of the Conference on the Use of Stimulant Drugs in the Treatment of Behaviorally Disturbed Young School Children, Sponsored by the Office of Child Development and the Office of the Assistant Secretary for Health and Scientific Affairs, Department of Health, Education and Welfare, Washington, D.C., January 11-12, 1971.

CHAPTER TWELVE

MARKS OF DISTINCTIVE TEACHING

Regular and special teachers are required for virtually every school today because each educational facility has its quota of youngsters needing special help.

It is extremely important that each student be in a learning situation where he is able to succeed adequately according to his intellectual, emotional, physical and social level—or where he can succeed according to intellectual level despite physical and/or social or emotional handicaps or lacks.

Special educational training can be provided a needy child in various places. They include:

1 School
   a. The regular classroom teacher
   b. A special education teacher

2 A private training center for special education.

3 Resources both in and outside the school who will work together on behalf of the child when such a dual program is needed.

Public schools today offer many kinds of "Special Education" classes. The programs include a wide range of services. Some of them are included in the following list:

Educationally Handicapped (EH)

... for children whose IQ is within the normal range but who cannot learn adequately in the regular classroom.

Educable Mentally Retarded (EMR)

... for children whose IQ is not within the normal range.

Trainable Mentally Retarded (TMR)

... for children whose IQ is lower than the EMR level. Many of these require some form of institutional care.

Mentally Gifted Minor (MGM)

...for children with a superior or better IQ who need academic challenges and enrichment over and above that which is received in the regular classroom.

Deaf and Severely Hard of Hearing (DHH)

...for children otologically handicapped.

Orthopedically Handicapped or Orthopedic-Delicate (OH)

...for children requiring special care because of bone, muscle and joint difficulties which prevent them from keeping up with the physical demands of the regular classroom.

Aphasic

...for children who cannot speak and/or understand speech in an adequate manner.

Blind

...for those who must be taught by the Braille method.

Visually Handicapped

...for children who are partially sighted.

Development Center for Handicapped Minors

...A year-round program for the severely mentally retarded or the multiple handicapped child who is not eligible for other Special Educational Classes in the schools.

Cerebral Palsy

...for children who have this condition and cannot manage themselves in a regular class.

Multi-Handicapped

...for children who have more than one handicap and require added specialized help.

Many people associate the term "special education" only with classes for the mentally retarded. But the above list demonstrates that such classes involve a wide spectrum of specialized help for children with a wide variety of problems.

The admission requirements for each program are quite specific. The decision to admit or not to admit should be the responsibility of a committee of specialists in that particular field so that no person has to shoulder the decision alone. Many far-reaching effects hang on a single decision.

Children should receive the best education available for their particular needs. It is indeed gratifying to know that these special educational efforts are becoming available to more and more special youngsters with particular problems. To offer the best training, each program requires certified, dedicated teachers—both for regular students and for those in special classes.

Teachers have different abilities, aptitudes, training and experience. Certain qualities which are desirable for all teachers are absolutely mandatory for those involved in special education. Not every teacher has them.

If your career is teaching, face yourself squarely. Find out if you have those special qualities demanded. If you do not, admit the fact and then proceed to find help. Cultivate the traits and develop them well. If you cannot do it on your own, obtain advice, guidance and assistance. These inner changes will give you a greater sense of accomplishment, to say nothing of the satisfaction of being better able to communicate and to meet the needs of your students. They will most certainly notice the difference in you. In fact, they most likely will sense even your first steps toward improvement.

Changes take time. It's all a growth process that doesn't bloom overnight. Youngsters are most perceptive, often being aware of an adult's strong points and inadequacies more keenly than the adult himself.

Some teachers will find it difficult to change and a few will find it impossible, even though they have the will to try. What is true for teachers is true for everybody. All of us can improve to a certain extent. Those who cannot change, even when they try, should not feel guilty. Rather, they should make certain they are in a teaching situation for which they are best suited.

Desirable Traits for Teachers of Distinction*

Enthusiasm for teaching must be apparent. It need not be constantly outward, but must be there undergirding a teacher's performance every day.

---

*Gathered from two sources: 1   Jack Eagon, Principal, Tracy Elementary School & Educationally Handicapped Admissions and Discharge Committee Board Member, 1965-1970, Baldwin Park, California; 2   Frank C. Pearce (1968).

Patience in trying circumstances. A teacher must remain calm and composed even when under fire from short or drawn-out problems. Consistent behavior is mandatory. A teacher shouldn't let the students know that they can get under his skin, even if they can!

Understanding of another's feelings. A good teacher takes the time to find out how he can help a child with a particular problem. Mutual respect is a good basis for it.

Flexibility in varied demands. A good teacher is able to help each student in as many different ways as possible when demands arise. He is not stereotyped and does not require his pupils to fit into his mold. He must be able to accept all students at *their* level of academic performance and behavior regardless of race, color or creed. He accepts youngsters that are unkempt, untidy, belligerent, sulky, tense, explosive, unhappy, withdrawn and lacking in self esteem.

Stamina for the demanding pace. Good physical and mental health is necessary for the teacher expecting to cope with the spontaneous situations that arise in the classroom.

Insight into all situations and the ability to determine: "Why is it a problem?"

Motivation in his responsibility to correct a problem in the best interest of the student. Good teachers have an extreme inner desire to serve the handicapped, basing their zeal on the true worth of all individuals.

Knowledge concerning . . .

1 What can solve the problem, what expertise, practical aids, and assistance are provided and how they can be adapted to the individual in a training program.

2 How much time to give a special problem.

A teacher must know instinctively how much time to devote to a special student. He must determine whether the sacrifice on his time is too great, robbing other students of their just due, and when special assistance is needed. The teacher must know if he has the ego strength to tackle the problem or if he needs help outside the classroom. He can become part of a larger team that is seeking the best educational setup for each student.

Humor for difficult circumstances. Handicapped youngsters, particularly those neurologically and/or emotionally involved, tend to be explosive, tense and abrupt in their mood swings. A teacher's sense of humor will keep many difficult situations from becoming major problems. Keen discernment is needed because some situations must be handled with gravity, not humor.

Creativity of teachers is taxed sometimes to the limit. Situations arise that challenge the teacher to use his ability to imagine and devise new ways to seek solutions. A teacher should take a chance and have the fortitude to try over and over again.

A balanced blend of good qualities will communicate to students that a teacher possesses a positive, meaningful attitude toward them. Until they feel that, students will not be able to learn adequately.

Dr. Burks (1968), has a concise chapter on the characteristics and skills of special class teachers.

A regular teacher is trained to handle a class of students with a normal range of IQ. Regular teaching techniques should be sufficient to help these students to learn what is being taught. However, every classroom has a cross-section of varying learning abilities which can be divided as follows:

1   A large group composed of students for whom the teaching program and rate of teaching is quite suitable.

2   A small group of slow learners for whom the classroom program is too advanced.

3   A handful of students for whom the classwork schedule is too slow—the mentally gifted.

Regular teachers with 25 to 40 students or more in a classroom do not have the time—and many do not have the specialized training and experience—to help slow learners, the mentally gifted, or other types of specialized students. Often the attitude of a regular teacher toward students with learning problems is reflected by the rest of the class. Children will do and follow more of what adults *do* than what adults *say*. When they observe that a teacher has the ego strength necessary to handle difficulties that learning problems create and can come up with humor rather than bitterness and with solutions rather than further complications, then most of them will do the same.

Occasionally a class will have that rare teacher who is rigid and who expects the same from each pupil *regardless*. In this classroom a child with learning disability has a tough assignment.

Once a teacher with such characteristics ridiculed an overactive, hard-to-manage child in front of the entire class by holding up a bottle of medicine his parents had sent to school for his daily lunch-time dosage.

"Our favorite troublemaker has finally got a pill to help him," the teacher said. "I wonder if it will do him any good."

The class laughed. The youngster felt bad enough about his learning-behavior problem but after that he was crushed by the cynical rejection led by the teacher and copied by the entire class.

Can you imagine the effect upon the class towards any pupil taking medication for a learning-behavior problem? Later on a physician may need to prescribe medication for another child in that classroom. Do you think he would be very cooperative about taking medicine after such callous remarks by his teacher?

Perhaps the teacher reacted from guilt feelings which grew out of her inability to handle that boy. When outside help was obtained by the parents she was reminded further of her inability to cope with her pupil. Her ego was simply too weak to rise above the situation and act maturely. She needed only to realize that the boy needed extra help and that she was not expected to give it alone. She might have acted differently had she seen the entire picture.

Part of professional excellence in any career is a realization of self capabilities and limitations. The professional person must know what he can do and where he must stop. When faced with a problem whose solution is beyond him one swallows his pride and refers the case to someone who is equipped to deal with the matter. In the case of a teacher, his ego is boosted later when the news comes that his child has been helped . . . and that he made the right decision in seeking added help.

How can a teacher assist medical follow-up?

After medication has been prescribed, a physician depends upon the teacher(s) to report to him through the parents on the effectiveness of the medicine. He wants to know its effectiveness on the child's learning and social situations in school. The report can be conveyed by phone or written down on a preprinted form which calls for answers to specific items and saves the teacher's time. See the author's short form in the appendix. A teacher rating scale has been developed by Dr. Conners (1969) for evaluating the effects of medication.

How can medication assist the teacher?

Good teaching requires effort and preparation. Each of us has his quota of energy each day, no more. When some of this energy is diverted from teaching to corral, prod, guide or throttle a child with learning disabilities that much less energy is diverted from teaching normal students.

At the mid-afternoon bell, school is out—for the children, not for the teacher. He must prepare lessons for the following day. If he is worn down by his hyperactive pupils his body and mind are too weary and he can't give his best to the next day's work. Inevitably the day for such a teacher comes when he cries, "That's it! I've had it! No more . . ."

An auto mechanic can't repair an engine that's running. Why should a teacher be expected to teach a student whose "engine" is accelerated? When medication slows down a hyperactive child, causing his nervous system to run at proper levels, the pupil's attention, concentration and retention capabilities are more normal and he can learn with his peers. The teacher finishes the day without exhaustion, fit and eager for another round next morning.

Teachers for specialized education are not easily found. Even if they were, such specialists should be spared unnecessary stress when proper medication for the student can easily eliminate it. Medicine, by helping the student, indirectly aids the teacher.

Occasionally, parents ask the personnel in special education classes to dismiss their children and put them back in the regular classroom. Such requests usually are made by parents emotionally motivated rather than by parents who face the facts.

Here is how specialists should deal with such requests:

Preventive measures

1   Before a pupil is placed in a special class his parents should understand completely the student's problem and understand how the special program will meet his educational needs. A parental visit to the special class is in order. The father should make every effort to leave work and join the mother for a visit.

2   Special education classes must be kept up to date with a meaningful program and a trained teacher. They must not be "baby-sitting" situations. If their child makes progress in the class his parents are less apt to request a change.

Active measures

1   Offer parents a complete explanation of their child's educational problem and how the class is meeting it. Outline clearly the frustrations that will be encountered in regular class work because of the child's inadequate learning, behavioral and emotional factors.

2   If the above is not convincing to parents, compare the child's achievement in class with that of another pupil (but withhold the name) who is the same age but in regular class. Then the parents can see for themselves how much of a gap really exists. This will convince most parents that a regular class is not the place for their youngster.

How can teachers alter behavior and performance?

Through training and experience, each instructor has various means and incentives to encourage his pupils to work and behave better. Some don't respond to the teacher's "bag of tricks," leaving the instructor more frustrated than ever.

Behavior Modification Techniques for teachers can come to the rescue in many cases. The school psychologist can too. His assistance can help the teacher to understand the principles involved as well as the appropriate application of techniques for the pupil(s) in question. Those techniques are progressive so that as each level of improved behavioral response is achieved there is the next level to attain for further emotional growth.

Behavior can also be modified by Contingency Management (Homme 1971, Sloane and Allen 1971). The basic difference between Contingency Management Behavior Modification is brought out by Leonard Krasner (1971) in his review, "Token Economy in the Classroom."

Both the California Association for the Neurologically Handicapped Child (CANHC) and the Association for Children with Learning Disabilities (ACLD) have literature departments that can supply additional information.

Dr. Burks (1968) has several worthwhile pointers on classroom control.

Recommended resource books include:

Glasser, William, *Schools Without Failure,* Harper & Row, New York, Evanston, London, 1969.

Lazarus, A. A., *Behavior Therapy and Beyond,* McGraw-Hill, New York, 1971.

Patterson, G. R., and **Gullion,** M. Elizabeth, *Living with Children: New Methods for Parents and Teachers,* revised edition, Champaign, Illinois, Research Press, 1971.

Smith, J., and **Smith,** E. P., *Child Management—A Program for Parents and Teachers,* University of Michigan, Ann Arbor, Mich.

Valett, R. E., *Modifying Child's Behavior: A Guide for Professionals,* Pacemaker Books, Fearon Publishers, Palo Alto.

Valett, R. E., *The Remediation of Learning Disabilities, A Handbook of Psychoeducational Resource Programs,* Fearon Publishers, Palo Alto, California 1967.

Yates, A. J., *Behavior Therapy,* John Wiley, New York, 1970.

Those desiring detailed guidance for carrying out the various perceptual training techniques may consult the following references suggested by Jack Schaeffer* who has demonstrated considerable success in the application of these techniques.

*Director of the Reading Guidance Institute, Whittier, California.

Agronowitz, Aleen and **McKeown,** Milfred Riddle, *Aphasia Handbook for Adults and Children,* Chas. Thomas Publishers, Springfield, Ill., 1964.

Ayres, A. Jean, The Development of Perceptual-Motor Abilities, *American Journal of Occupational Therapy,* Vol. XVIV, No. 6, 1963.

Cruickshank, William M., *A Teaching Method for Brain Injured and Hyperactive Children,* Syracuse University Press, 1961.

Dubnoff, Belle and **Chambers,** Irene, Perceptual Training as a Bridge to Conceptual Ability, *Educational Therapy,* Special Child Publications of the Sequin School, Inc., Seattle, Washington, 1966.

Dubnoff, Belle and **Fargo,** George, Aspects of Perceptual Training with Brain Injured and Emotionally Disturbed Children as Related to Reading, Claremont Reading Conference, 25th Yearbook, Claremont University College, Claremont, California, 1961.

Kephart, N. C., *The Slow Learner in the Classroom,* Charles E. Merrill Books, Inc., 1960.

Montessori, Maria, *Spontaneous Activity in Education,* Schoken Books, New York, 1965.

Myklebust, Helmer R., *Auditory Disorders in Children,* Grune and Stratton, New York, 1954.

Strauss, A. A., and **Lehtinen,** L. E., *Psychopathology and Education of the Brain Injured Child,* Grune and Stratton, Inc., 1947.

Van Witsen, Betty, *Perceptual Training Activities Handbook,* TC Series in Special Education, Teachers College Press, Columbia University, New York, 1967.

Zweig, Richard L. and **Bruno,** Muriel E., Teachers' Instructional Manual for Remedial Reading Laboratory, Califone, Div. of Rheem Mfg. Co., Los Angeles, California, 1966.

Are all EMRs truly EMR?

Some children classified as "Educable Mentally Retarded" definitely are not so. These pupils should be in a different type of class—regular or "educational handicap." They most likely will belong in a class situation between "EMR" and "EH" rather than in a regular class. Some call this group a "transitional class."

There is a way to recognize and evaluate these pseudo-EMRs. The informed EMR teacher may observe that a certain child shows flashes of intelligence above that of the usual EMR student, and that the pupil seems to have ability but just cannot seem to harness it consistently. Self criticism, for example, is not a normal feature of a typical EMR. This is manifested, for example, by crying caused by frustration arising from trying too hard to accomplish a task he is certain he can do. Any

EMR student who can think abstractly should be further evaluated and helped because he might well be a pseudo type.

In one public school there were two EMR pupils who were quite hyperactive and who often upset the entire class. Their teacher asked if something could be done to reduce this behavior and thus help both the EMRs and the class. A neurological examination revealed some of the typical coordination, balance, and perceptual problems. During the testing the students were more responsive and alert than one would expect from the EMR type. Medication was recommended which proved effective enough so that a retesting of the IQ was carried out. The results took the pupils out of the EMR range. One child was placed in the EH class and the other in regular class!

The percentage of pseudo EMRs is small. But for those who can be helped the discovery is a dramatic turn toward wonderful advancement.

Some true EMRs can be helped to achieve even more where they are and to get the maximum value out of their IQ after medical and perceptual help is applied.

Similarly, some hyperactive Trainable Mentally Retarded children can be helped by proper medication not only for behavior control but also for increased learning potential.

BIBLIOGRAPHY FOR CHAPTER TWELVE

Burks, Harold F., Treatment Procedures: Selection and Training of Special Class Teachers, *Burks Behavior Rating Scale for Organic Brain Dysfunction,* pp. 100-102, Arden Press, El Monte, California, 1968.
Ibid., Principles of Classroom Control, pp. 82-87.

Conners, C.K., A Teacher Rating Scale for Use in Drug Studies with Children, *American Journal of Psychiatry,* Vol. 126, No. 6, pp. 152-156, December, 1969.

Homme, Lloyd E., Human Motivation and Environment, *An Empirical Basis for Change in Education, Selections on Behavioral Psychology for Teachers,* edited by **Becker,** Wesley C., chapter 21, pp. 26, 274, Science Research Associates, Inc., Chicago, Palo Alto, 1971.

Krasner, Leonard, Behavior Therapy: Positive Reinforcement, Token Economy in the Classroom, *Annual Review of Psychology,* edited by **Farnsworth,** P.R., Annual Reviews, Palo Alto, Calif., pp. 498-499, 1971.

Pearce, Frank C., Seven Needed Qualities of a Basic Educational Teacher, *Adult Leadership,* Vol. 16, No. 7, pp. 255-ff., 1968.

Sloane, Howard N., Jr., and **Allen,** John E., An In-Service Teacher Training Program in Contingency Management, *An Empirical Basis for Change in Education, Selections on Behavioral Psychology for Teachers,* edited by **Becker,** Wesley C., chapter 29, pp. 375-397, Science Research Associates, Inc., Chicago, Palo Alto, 1971.

CHAPTER THIRTEEN

A PERSONAL WORD TO PARENTS

Mothers and fathers of handicapped children are special. They have been called upon by their circumstances both to bear an added burden and to achieve heights of achievement unknown to others.

Parents who must handle the task of helping a child with a special problem are not alone in their struggle. The resources of many agencies and professional personnel are at their disposal. Such resources have not always been available, causing many parents much frustration.

The goal of good parents is to assist their child in reaching full normal growth and development so he can become a mature, competent adult. One of the purposes of this book is to acquaint parents with the broad aspects of learning disabilities, a few of which may apply in their case. Thus fortified, parents will have less difficulty adjusting to a problem whose cause and cure they can more fully understand.

When a parent discovers the learning disabilities of his child he finds himself in a variety of situations. Here are two extremes:

1   The parent searches for community help on behalf of his youngster but can find none. No local medical, educational or psychological professional knows what to do (Wender and Eisenberg 1971, Colodny, Kenny and Kurlander 1968). Or, if they know about the problem intellectually they haven't enough practical experience to initiate help.

2   At the other end of the range of possibilities is a parent who, after inquiring, learns that various facilities are operational in the school district and privately in the community but that they are not in a position to know what the child really needs and what steps to take to locate proper help. This situation is like a person dying of thirst near cactus plants in the desert, not knowing he could have obtained liquid from the prickly weed and lived.

Finances regulate the degree of help a family can provide. But even if finances are available, that doesn't guarantee that help can be found. Medical and psychological facilities in some areas are uninformed about what to do for children with varying degrees of learning disabilities. If this is the case, here is a suggested plan of action.

Ask your physician if he would like information on your child's problem that you could share with him. No one likes to have information shoved in his face or forced on him. But if the person is first *asked* then he can invite the exchange of information.

Channel your enthusiasm for helping your child with tact and good taste. We humans move slowly until new and controversial matters are fully established. Change and adjustment to new things are difficult and awkward at first. Even some professional people are at first against tested methods for helping learning disabilities in children. Others are immediately for them. Still others halt between two opinions because they have insufficient facts.

As a parent, you want desperately to help your child. Therefore, continue to search for those people in your community who are open minded, patient and flexible. With them you will be able to share what you have learned helps your child best. Do not settle for that worn-out cliche: "You're just an overanxious parent; the child is fine. I'm sure he'll outgrow it." Another annoying comment is: "Your child is immature." That, usually, is where their judgment stops. They neglect to say *why* your child is immature. So thank them for their help and opinions but keep searching.

Remember, most worthwhile things in life are worth working for—hard! Your investment in your child is worth all the effort you expend. You will not lose your reward.

Should parents blame heredity?

The heredity factor plays a major role in causing learning disabilities, but the line is traced not just to parents. It can go far down the family tree to recent or distant generations past. No one, really, is to blame. But the parents are definitely to blame who will not do all within their power to assist a child with problems if it lies within their power to do so.

Just how important is parental involvement?

Special educational teachers and administrators make a very strong point that the parents' involvement is a must for progress in learning even in the best run special programs.

"Obvious" situations are not always "true" situations

Parents often charge: "He's not trying!" or "She doesn't want to learn!" or "The child is just mean."

Stop and think a moment: Who would continue trying to walk up a slippery hillside if each attempt caused the individual to slide back and fall down? Children don't like failure. Do you? It's rare for a person to continue a pursuit that spells failure. Thus it is natural for a child to cease trying, to withdraw from school, to develop psychosomatic headaches, stomach aches, etc., so he can avoid the failure-factory.

Your child wants to learn! He is more eager to learn than you are to have him learn. His bad behavior is a normal reaction to frustration. He knows he should be learning but since he can't, bad behavior is his way of saying, "Look at me! I've got a learning problem. I need help! Please help me!"

Here is another way to look at it, to see how bad or abnormal behavior develops from a learning problem.

Everyone desires success and attention. Both are accomplished as a person uses his inherent ability to achieve good or positive success and good or positive attention. Those with learning disabilities find it difficult to gain good success and good attention because of their handicap.

Darkness is the absence of light; cold is the absence of heat; and bad success or failure results when good success is unattainable. To most people, success is attaining a favorable goal. A person who attains an illegal or illegitimate goal is "successful" in his own eyes, even though he has achieved negative or bad success.

Since all human beings need attention they'll get it by good methods or bad. The disabled pupil says unconsciously, "I can't get my parents' and teachers' attention with good grades, but I'll get their attention!" He resorts to disruptive or manipulative behavior or "acting out."

Boys become quite successful in a negative sort of way, at attracting attention. They fight, stage temper outbursts, or become the class clown. Girls tease, stick out their tongues, indulge in name calling, make a scene, become a tomboy, fight and show temper tantrums too.

Lies are common because they hide the faults of a weak ego or self concept. Stealing is another negative success item. It's amazing what people will do to get attention at any cost. Some become successful in turning off the world about them as they withdraw into themselves.

Many children and teenagers identify with this basic explanation of positive and negative aspects concerning success and attention.

Taking specific instances out of their case histories and daily lives helps them to see the mechanism of how they will automatically substitute the negative when the positive cannot be achieved. In realizing this they see that the bad success item isn't really helping them but only harms them. This causes them to think twice before carrying on with further negative success actions.

Most children and teenagers appreciate being told "how it is" and the logical and reasonable explanations for their learning and behavior problems. The truth about themselves may be difficult to accept, or be hard to understand, and may even hurt their feelings. But this is of no lasting consequence when they know their problem is being understood with acceptance, patience and skill that holds promise for something better in the future.

Why do some parents fear "special" classes?

Parents want the best for their children. They long to see healthy bodies, sound minds and fervent spirits in their offspring. A "regular class," they feel, is the only place where their child can achieve his goals. They also feel that a "special class" reflects on the child's poor mentality and obliquely on the family or directly on the parent.

Parents with such views should consider what is involved in "special classes." Is it not wonderful that educators have organized special programs for special needs? Other parents organized themselves and have aided in the establishment of these programs. Without it, pupils in this kind of learning situation may develop further physical, emotional, social, educational and spiritual complications that will make life a burden to themselves and to others.

Isn't it wonderful that dedicated teachers are willing to face the challenge of these special classes? When parents see the issue in perspective, they will be better prepared to ignore or accept the social stigma and the heartache that sometimes accompany the situation and begin to appreciate the specialized training available to their children. The pupils will be able to progress and succeed at their rate and level of achievement, rather than to struggle along in a regular class for ego's sake where frustration and failure are the inevitable result. A youngster's present progress and future achievement count more in the long run than uneasy parental feelings during the specialized training.

Need "special" classes be the only way?

A few school districts no longer have "special" segregated classes, but integrate the learning disability child in the regular classroom. This requires new methods or systems employing the assistance of educational specialists and the cooperative effort of the entire school staff. One such district is generating a lot of interest of late, due to their success with the integrated system.

How can parents reduce anxiety and misgivings?

By seeking additional information from school authorities, parents can relax with a sort of "all-overish" knowledge of the situation. This leads to calm decisions. A school principal or someone in the Special Education Department will gladly arrange an appointment. Parents are allowed to observe a special class in most schools and to discuss and ask questions of teachers concerning their child. Opportunity is also afforded to meet the parents of other children in the special class.

Where can parents meet other couples with similar problems?

Social, county, state and national organizations have meetings which parents can attend. Membership in such groups can be rewarding.

The California Association for the Neurologically Handicapped Child (CANHC), for example, functions for the benefit of parent, child, teacher and other interested parties. A similar organization serving other states is the Association for Children with Learning Disabilities (ACLD). These two groups fill an important need for parents whose children are in specialized education programs.

Local chapters have meetings at which parents meet other parents and share their experiences. They see films, listen to speakers, and learn about literature, methods, and other resources available to meet the problems of children.

What if no local organization exists?

If there is no such agency in your area, start one! "Necessity," said a wise person, "is the mother of invention." Write or phone the regional or state headquarters of CANHC[1] if you live in California, or write to ACLD[2] if you live in another state. Ask your local PTA president to arrange a program on learning disabilities during a regular PTA session. This will attract other parents needing and/or looking for similar help. Many organizations have been organized simply because parents find that they have neighbors and friends with like needs.

What attitudes and attributes should these parents have?

Patience and understanding are at the top of the list. Next comes flexibility in handling children with learning disabilities. Parents can be like some school teachers who try to force all children into the same mold.

---

1   The address of the California Association for the Neurologically Handicapped Child is P.O. Box 604, Main Office, Los Angeles, Calif., 90053.

2   The address of the Association for Children with Learning Disabilities is 2200 Brownsville Rd., Pittsburgh, Pa. 15210. Both CANHC and ACLD have literature departments that can supply additional material.

But it's usually true: the same children in the same family under the same roof have different and varied needs—even though learning disabilities are not involved. Parents must be consistent in discipline and of one mind. Punish a child for bad behavior at home or at school but *never punish him for poor school work!* Instead, find out the true causes of his learning difficulties.

Can a parent over-react dangerously?

When a person sees in another his own undesirable traits he reacts against those idiosyncracies more strongly. In the case of parent against child, the mother or father tends to punish more severely. He or she may even become quite angry, hostile and lose his or her temper. No one would punish himself for a past or present behavior. But if it happens to his own children—watch out!

This observation is particularly true of fathers and their sons. There is a high male incidence in the hereditary factor so it's not surprising that dad takes out his disappointments on his son and the learning difficulty.

A frustrated dad usually reacts in two ways: Either he will become very defensive because of his male ego, pride and guilt over the same type of problem and declare, "There's nothing wrong with my son—he's just a normal boy . . . a regular guy!" Or he will over-punish, pick on his son and make him feel more inferior than ever. The dad who cannot accept himself will have difficulty accepting his son.

Can psychological counseling help parents?

There is a reason for a person's behavior—whatever it might be. Anyone who cannot properly relate to his own flesh and blood should find out why. By seeking help, the cause(s) can be more quickly found and the remedy initiated.

When a troubled child sees his parents' attitudes change from negative to positive he experiences a tremendous uplift. When hostility is replaced by patience, and when love and understanding take the place of anger, what a boost to all concerned! As adults we want to act like mature people. One true barometer of love is the ability to love another not necessarily because the other pleases us but because he is a person. This is the trait children most want to see and feel in parents.

Even parents who are quite well balanced emotionally should seek counsel if they have a handicapped child. The sessions with a specialist will help them to understand their child much better.

*What happens to a child who is disciplined without love, or vice versa?**

Maximum control and maximum love causes a child to feel *over-pro-tected*.

When parents exercise minimum control and maximum love the child becomes *spoiled*.

PARENTAL INFLUENCES

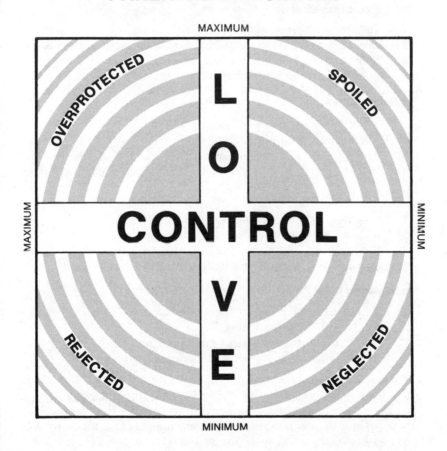

*Diagram and answer used by permission from unpublished material by Newton S. Metfessal, Ph.D., Professor of Educational Psychology, University of Southern California, Los Angeles, California.

Maximum parental control or discipline with minimal love causes a child to feel *rejected.*

When parental control is minimal and love is minimal the child feels *neglected.*

When love and control are proportionately balanced, this procedure offers the greatest potential for developing a normal child.

The four unbalanced types develop the following symptoms:

The Overprotected Child

1 Tends to reject responsibility.
2 Develops anxiety in meeting people and in facing new experiences.
3 Prefers to be a follower most of his life.
4 Prefers not to think for himself.

The Spoiled Child

1 Has difficulty making and keeping friends.
2 Becomes more and more demanding and selfish.
3 Tends to respond to restrictions with outbreaks of temper.
4 Wants to get his way by charm, wheedling, coaxing and bullying.

The Rejected Child

1 Lacks feelings of security or sense of belonging.
2 Tends to become aggressive, resentful and quarrelsome.
3 Often acquires behavior to get attention.
4 Generally develops non-conformity toward social standards.

The Neglected Child

1 May later develop little emotional reaction to others.
2 Usually will be without direction.
3 May continue to have serious emotional problems.
4 Often fails to develop a sense of right and wrong.

Raising a "spoiled brat" (or any other of the following types listed) is a lot easier than you may think. Simply follow the suggestions given. Who knows, you may already have progressed further than you realize! If this is the case, it's not yet too late to change. (The following was prepared in collaboration with Ernest Schellenberg, Ed.D., a clinical psychologist.)

The Overprotected Child—the result of excessive control and excessive love.

• Be an over-indulgent parent.

- Make all the child's decisions (even the ones he knows how to make).
- Answer all questions asked the child by others (don't even let the child give the answers he or she knows how to give).
- Force your child as completely as possible into your mold and don't allow him to be himself.
- Make excuses for any and all wrongs of the child.
- Cover up or overlook any and all failures of the child.
- When a younger child does something wrong you should regard the child as having done something cute.

Example: This type of parent would insist on music lessons or certain clothes for the child regardless of how the child felt, reacted or however he objected.

The Spoiled Child—the result of lack of control and excessive love.
- Allow your child to get by with anything.
- Never think of directing or guiding the child and never make a decision for him or her, especially the ones he or she cannot make.
- Be sure to give in to the child so he always gets his way. After all, you want him to grow up hating himself and at the same time learning how to manipulate adults.

Example. This type of parent couldn't care less whether the child took music lessons or not. He would allow the child to wear whatever clothes the youngster wanted.

The Rejected Child—the result of excessive control and lack of love.
- Be a severe disciplinarian. (Have rules and regulations for everything the child does or might do. Punishment is quick, firm and impressive.)
- Be sure you seldom give praise for doing right.
- Remind (better yet, nag) the child often about the wrongs he has done.
- Keep an adequate distance between you and the child. After all, "Children are to be seen and not heard."
- Give as little indication as possible that you love the child or that you want him around you.

Example: This type of parent would either punish the child or nag him for errors made in the music lessons even while practicing. When the child would perform well the parent would in a begrudging manner give a small amount of praise, but might add, "It's about time," or "I did much better when I was your age."

The Neglected Child—the result of lack of control and lack of love (fortunately, this sort of child is uncommon).

• Be apathetic.

• Leave the child entirely to itself (this type is often the offspring of schizophrenic parents).

Example: This type of parent figures (if at all) that the child is "just there, so what?"

What can be done at home to alter behavior?

Teachers use "Behavior Modification Techniques" in the classroom, but similar methods are designed for use by parents in the home.

To carry out these techniques parents must be in full agreement and cooperate mutually. If either parent is inconsistent or if there is inconsistency between the parents, the child will be one of the first to spot it and the poor behavior will not change for the better. The child will even use this disagreement for further manipulation.

Among the resource references are:

Modifying Children's Behavior, by Robert E. **Valett,** Pacemaker Books, Fearon Publishers, Palo Alto, California 94300.

Living with Children: New Methods for Parents and Teachers, Revised edition. G. R. **Patterson,** and M. Elizabeth **Gullion,** Research Press 1971, Champaign, Illinois 61820.

Improving Your Child's Behavior, by Madeline C. **Hunter** and Paul V. **Carlson,** TIP Publications, El Segundo, California 90245.

Child Management—a Program for Parents by Judith M. **Smith,** M.A. and Donald E. P. **Smith,** Ph.D. Ann Arbor Publishers, 610 Forest, Ann Arbor, Michigan 48104.

Parents Are Teachers: a child management program by Wesley C. **Becker,** Research Press, 1971.

For Love of Children, Behavioral Psychology for Parents, by Roger W. **McIntire,** Ph.D., CRM Books, 1970, Del Mar, California 92014.

A Parent's Guide to Learning Problems, by Margaret **Golick,** Quebec ACLD, Montreal, Canada.

Of what value are regular, non-specialized private schools for handicapped children?

For the most part, private secular, Catholic or Protestant schools are not designed or equipped to handle special educational problems. Most of these schools have a higher academic level when compared grade for grade with public schools. Therefore a pupil who is already achieving below the normal grade level in public school will become further behind in a private school.

Some parents feel their child will receive more personalized attention in private school because classes are smaller. This is often true, but in some private schools the classes are jammed with more than 40 students. Parents must check out the situation before registering their children in private schools.

Small classes are desirable, but even 20 or 22 pupils in a class is too many for a child with a learning disability. In addition, such children need a teacher who has taken special training for educating the educationally handicapped.

The author's experience in Southern California shows that public school districts are much better equipped and programmed with special teachers than are the regular private schools.

Are there private specialized schools for problem learners?

This kind of school is available. Two of the best known in Southern California are The Marianne Frostig Center of Educational Therapy, and the Dubnoff School for Educational Therapy.

Both CANHC and ACLD can assist parents in finding others in the various states.

Can a child attend a special perceptual remedial reading clinic successfully and not make progress in school work?

Ted was such a boy. While in the fifth grade he was enrolled at a clinic and tested at second level. In eight months he progressed nicely and was reading at fourth-grade level. But his parents noted that this progress was not mirrored in his school work.

Although the boy gained in reading ability he was unable to "regain" all the reading content he had missed during that two-year span of troubled learning. His teacher still expected him to work out of a fifth grade book, reasoning: "After all, he is fifth-grade age!" But the fifth grade book for Ted was still one year ahead of his newly attained reading ability. Obviously, adjustments had to be made and fast.

Working with children is a rewarding challenge. It takes effort, consistent follow-through, money and time. Sometimes the visible results don't come as quickly as one would like. But for most earnest seekers after normalcy, results do come in ample quantity and in time.

Parents are the key figures in a child's life. They must open his doors to life's correct paths. Many doors can be opened by a child alone; but problem doors he must allow specialists to open, in cooperation with the parents. Knowing what the problem is removes many of the fears and anxieties that first result.

One of the aims of this chapter has been to enlighten parents and then to guide them as they seek to ease the burden that parents and children are called upon to bear. For a job well done in this area, the rewards are sweet indeed.

BIBLIOGRAPHY FOR CHAPTER THIRTEEN

Colodny, Dorothy, **Kenny,** Carolyn, and **Kurlander,** L.F., The Educationally Handicapped Child: The Physician's Place in a Program to Overcome Learning Disability. *California Medicine,* Vol. 109, No. 1, pp. 15-18, California Medical Association, July, 1968.

Wender, Paul H., foreword by **Eisenberg,** Leon, *Minimal Brain Dysfunction in Children,* pp. ix, x, Wiley-Interscience, a Division of John Wiley & Sons, Inc., New York, 1971.

CHAPTER FOURTEEN

THE STRATEGY OF COUNSELING

Counseling services given on behalf of students by the school psychologist, psychiatrist, or clinical psychologist play an important role in the program of assistance to the whole pupil.

This personalized aid can be beneficial to several people simultaneously:

1 The child

2 The parents (even mother alone, if father refuses, or vice versa)

3 The teacher, in both regular and special classrooms

Although a child may not be counseled directly by the school psychologist because of a lack of time, the young person receives the benefit of his advice through the program he sets up for the teacher. Instructors can better understand a pupil with learning disabilities when they observe the results of psychological testing and the interpretations thereof.

An IQ profile, for example, gives the teacher information about the child's strong points and areas needing improvement. It shows what general achievement levels could be expected.

Projective testing offers clues to the emotional state of the child. Visual, auditory, and tactile perceptual tests help to convince a teacher that special help is needed and then to guide him in preparing for it.

The psychologist can work closely with the teacher in setting various Behavior Modification Techniques for a certain pupil and then in following through to see that it's done.

Another helpful program is the "parent effectiveness" group meetings held either at school or in a home. These give parents the proper insight concerning their child's problem and why the youngster behaves as he does . . . why he has difficulty learning when all the other siblings are doing fine. These meetings offer suggestions on how to handle discipline in the home, how to regulate situations so that frustrations don't become overwhelming, how to aid the parent in explaining to the other children that special attention for one of their number is needed because of a learning problem. Behavior Modification Techniques for parents, as well as for teachers, have been worked out. It's nice to have guidance in putting them into practice. The techniques must be carried out correctly to achieve meaningful results.

One of counseling's main goals is to help people to see their, or someone else's, problems beyond the obvious. A skilled psychologist can help parents and children discover *why* the subject is doing what he's doing. When that is established, the cause can be determined. When the cause is determined a change or modification can be prescribed and carried out.

In most situations, it takes brains to get into trouble. Often trouble is a child's method of getting attention, even though he knows punishment will follow. Counseling helps parents and teachers to know what's really going on. The trouble-maker is most likely acting out with bad behavior to get attention. Hopefully, someone will take note and find out the underlying true cause of his problem and correct it. After that's accomplished the child can attain good success with his ability and elicit good attention. Dr. Burks (1968) groups fourteen traits of the "acting out" (functionally disturbed) child and fourteen traits of the "acting up" (hyperkinetic) child and then compares them. Children can have traits from both lists. These lists can aid in determining the main groupings and thus act as a guide in the treatment program.

We all crave attention from others. We were made to give and receive proper attention. Some need special assistance both to give it and to receive it. Most children with learning disabilities are involved with behavior problems, however the primary cause of it is usually in the form of minimal brain dysfunction. Counseling is not intended to correct a neurological problem and should not be expected to do so. In this connection the comment of Dr. Sam Clements, Ph.D. is startling: "Seventy-five per cent of the emotional problems presented to school psychologists had their basis and beginning in learning disabilities." It is important here to recall the high incidence of learning problems that are neurological in origin.

Counseling is required to build up a weak or poor self-image. Who likes to feel inferior? The building of an adequate self-concept from a human standpoint is dependent upon two basic factors:

1   Does the person himself achieve adequately at his own level of ability so as to have a proper reaction of self-acceptance, self-worth, and self-competence?

2   Do parents, family, teacher and peers accept the person, making him feel genuinely worthy and do they show that they have confidence in him?

A learning disability makes it difficult in varying degrees for these two factors to function. When one or the other or both do not take place, an emotional problem develops due to the inadequate self-image or self-concept. It is difficult for the troubled child to believe that others accept him, even though they really do, when he does not accept himself, because he has failed to reach his own level of ability.

What produces a low image of one's self? Here are three basic inadequacies that result in such a situation (Wagner):

1 An inadequate sense of acceptance, love and trust results in hostility, hate, malice, greed, feelings of rejection, selfishness, etc. A child who says, "No one loves me," is more than likely expressing his own feeling about himself. Adults who will not accept a child with problems produce this feeling in that child.

2 An inadequate sense of worth results in guilt. Most people associate guilt with wrongdoing. But it can also result from not being able to do what you expect of yourself or what others expect of you.

3 An inadequate sense of competence. This results in feelings of anxiety and fear. You couldn't do it before, you can't do it now, and you won't be able to do it in the future. The reason is that the child is already overanxious about past failure. New tasks make for even greater anxiety and fear because the threat is greater. How can a child in this frame of mind perform something new that is unfamiliar to him when he cannot perform the tasks at hand with which he is familiar?

When faced with these annoying inadequacies, it is small wonder that a child or adult veers to one side or the other away from the midline balance of normal emotions, acting out in bad behavior or becoming shy, listless or withdrawn. All this is an oversimplification of abnormal emotional reactions but it at least offers a basic framework of information to explain what can and does happen.

A good foundation takes time to build, even in an "instant" world where there is so much "easy come, easy go." *Not so fast and steady* is much better than *fast and faulty*. Rebuilding a weakened foundation takes longer to rebuild than the original, but the effort involved is worthwhile. People who need counseling on a regular private basis cannot be rushed through the process particularly when the major cause in the learning disability is emotional in origin, thus making counseling the primary means of treatment.

"Between the ages of five and ten the child forms his lifelong concept of himself as a success or as a failing person. . . ." (Glasser 1969).

The emotional development of our children is of primary importance. A proper understanding of how that development can be unfavorably altered by learning problems is paramount in the recognition and treatment of those problems.

BIBLIOGRAPHY FOR CHAPTER FOURTEEN

Burks, Harold F., Problems of Diagnosis, *Burks Behavior Rating Scale for Organic Brain Dysfunction,* chapter 12, p. 60, Arden Press, El Monte, California, 1968.

Glasser, William, *Schools without Failure,* Harper & Row, New York, 1969.

Wagner, Maurice, *The Building of an Adequate Self Concept,* Manuscript in preparation, Los Angeles, California.

CHAPTER FIFTEEN

COORDINATION DEVELOPMENT
AND PERCEPTUAL-MOTOR TRAINING

Another practical discipline that produces results among children with learning disabilities is the subject of coordination development and perceptual-motor training.

This important theory deals with the relationship of body movement to the academic learning process. The study gains further credence as research in this field continues to develop. Meaningful programs are bringing specific improvement to participants. Children with poor balance, poor fine and gross coordination, poor fine and gross body perception, impaired directionality, impaired laterality, poor rapid reversing ability, poor rhythm, poor position in space—these for the most part are also children who are underachievers in school. That fact is certainly not without significance. If the brain cannot adequately control fingers, thumbs, hands, feet, limbs and the rest of the body in a perceptual-motor fashion, even though they are physically connected to it, then it would seem logical that it would have the same or greater difficulty controlling the coordination of non-physical or less concrete information involved in the learning process in or out of school.

We are constantly learning. The amount of information varies only in degree and intensity. If the hand cannot correctly follow and carry out the orders of the will of the brain, how can the malfunctioning hand, which looks physically intact, be expected to relay to the brain what it senses? The interrelationship and interdependency of the paired sensory (afferent) nerves and motor (efferent) nerves of the body are established in neurophysiology.

Much of what we learn with our eyes and ears is reinforced for more complete learning when the sense of touch is brought into play. Seeing something "round" and hearing that it is "round" do not provide the full meaning. It is not really understood until one touches and feels the "round" object with the hand.

Notice how babies and children are constantly "touching" things as they grow and learn. Their parents are just as constantly scolding, "I said *look* at it; I didn't say *touch* it!"

We all learned that hot was hot not by being told but by the "ouch."

Experimentation in this area was done by R. Held and Hein using cats. A cat that was active and able to use its legs and paws, along with its eyes and ears, developed perception. But the passive animal using only eyes and ears but no legs and paws remained effectively blind.

These researchers suggested then that active touch is essential to perceptual development (Gregory 1966).

When a person does not properly perceive his own physical body it is unlikely he will perceive the world around him. Each of us is the center of our own world. Our perception, knowledge and interpretation of ourselves forms our basis for perceiving, knowing and interpreting the world around us. The brain is the central reference for everything in the person and therefore everything in his environment.

The expression "Charity begins at home" sums it up well. If one doesn't know how to love, respect and care for himself it is unlikely that he will do so for others.

This principle is true psychologically as well. "Emotional stability begins at home." If one isn't stable within himself he will not find stability around him.

Now add another truism: "Perception begins at home." The person who does not perceive his own physical self adequately will not perceive the world around him adequately. In many cases the environment does not make a person. It only reveals what they truly are. All of this emphasizes the basic need of having the physical portion of our total personality in the best perceptual-motor development order as possible according to one's maturational age.

John Tynes (1971), Director of Physical Education in the Placentia Unified School District, Placentia, California summarizes this aspect of research in, "This Is a Program that Works," found in the *Teacher's Guide: Perceptual-Motor Training Program.* Mr. Tynes states:*

> After working with more than 7,000 children over a three-year period, after studying the results of a major TITLE I study on the effectiveness of the program, after personally watching its influence upon many hundreds of individual children from kindergarten through sixth grade, and after talking with their teachers, parents, doctors and psychologists, I can say with some assurance: *This program works;* this program definitely upgrades children's coordination, body image, self concept, happiness, drive for learning, academic readiness and

*Used by permission.

academic performance. In particular, this program, to a high degree, has lifted the academic achievement of children who had learning difficulties.

We don't claim to cure anything. We don't claim to make dramatic improvements with every child. But we do teach improved perception and coordinated movement; and by and large, when these skills are lifted, so is academic performance. One sign of that here in Placentia, California is that after three years of perceptual-motor training, even though we will have one thousand more students in our school district next year, our special education classes will be smaller than they have been in the last ten years, for the simple reason that these children are being raised out of the need for special education and transferred into regular classes.

I encourage all teachers, all school districts and all professionals who work with children to structure a perceptual-motor training activity into their school program. I am sure it will pay results. Our local medical people believe in it, and we have some of the finest in the nation. Our psychologists believe in it, so do the college professors who have studied it. Some thirty-two elementary school districts in our area of Southern California now have adopted some type of perceptual-motor training, and they too are getting results.

But those results will come only if you give this neuromuscular training the importance it deserves, preferably with a period every day, at least two or three times a week. Make yourself knowledgeable in this exciting field. Begin the work with confidence, with patience, kindness—both with a smile and a sense of discipline.

Emphasize the importance of listening—your children must listen carefully to what you say and follow your directions. Give your children plenty of opportunities for success, for achievement—persist in a task until they can do it. Give them plenty of variety, a great many different ways to build their balance, their rhythm, their coordination, their perception of their bodies and of forms and shapes, their gross and fine motor control. Do that, and you will succeed: you will really help the children, and you will have one of the most rewarding teaching experiences of your life.

The following information is taken from the Introduction of the same *Teacher's Guide: Perceptual-Motor Training Program* (1971):*

Perceptual-Motor Training in Theory and Practice

One of the major discoveries made by academic and physical educators during the past decade is that all kinds of young children—with average, below-average, and above-average I.Q., achievers and non-achievers—can make substantial improvement in both mental and physical performance through a regular program of perceptual-motor training: a program that improves the child's ability to *perceive* the various stimuli in this environment, and to respond with full *"motor"* (muscular) control.

Consider the results from such programs:

Normal children have upgraded both their scholastic performance and physical coordination. Essentially normal children who were slow learners have increased their academic drive, learning skills and school achievement, shown by improved reading, writing, arithmetic. Otherwise normal children who had serious physical coordination problems have improved control of their bodies. Even handicapped children, including some who were retarded or brain-damaged, have made both academic and physical progress. And dispirited, emotionally disturbed children have boosted their self-image, social adjustment and personal happiness.

Perceptual-Motor Development

How is it that the repeated, rhythmic, coordination-improving movements of regularly-performed neuro-muscular exercise can produce such varied and impressive results?

Such scholars as Drs. Kephart, Getman and Frostig have found that a child's academic ability and his bodily coordination are inseparable from his *basic percep-*

*Used by permission.

tual-motor development. This development is shown in the child's ability to correctly *perceive* the stimuli received by his visual, auditory, tactile and kinesthetic or muscle senses, and to *respond* to these stimuli with appropriate, controlled gross and fine *motor* activities.

Basic perceptual-motor development is essential to the child's academic achievement and self-image. It can be approximated by observing the child's ability to identify the parts of his body, maintain balance on a walking beam, demonstrate coordination by skipping and hopping, draw such basic forms as circles and squares, and control eye movement by following a moving target.

Thus academic ability is seen as something more than a function of abstract intelligence or "mental capacity." It is seen as a developed skill in perceiving, and responding to, stimuli—a skill that requires basic ability in perception of one's self and one's environment, and in appropriate body management or control.

Seeing vs. Perceiving

While stimulus patterns are always present in the environment, it takes the perceptual mechanism to make sense of these stimuli—to organize and interpret them, to comprehend them as they actually are.

A child may have perfect sight but not see the difference between a "b" and a "d," or between a "q" and a "p." When such a child mistakes these letters, it is not because he is stupid or confused. To him there simply is no difference because his "laterality"—his inner sense of leftness and rightness—has not yet been developed:

Or the child's inability to perceive spatial differences may cause him to read "saw" as "was"—simply because he has no clear sense of his own vertical mid-line. He *sees* the "s" and "w" all right; but he does not *perceive* the whole word. He does not see that the "s" is on the left of the "a" and the "w" on the right. By the same token, the teacher may write "63" on the blackboard but the child may *see* "36."

Drawing a Square

Even after laterality is developed, and a child can *see*

the difference between similar-looking letters, he will not be able to *read* them in words and in sentences until his eyes have developed "tracking" ability (skill in quickly focusing and following from left to right on successive lines). And the child will not be able to *write* these letters and words until he has learned sufficient dexterity—of the fingers, wrist, arms, shoulders, the entire "grasp" mechanism. Many young school-age children simply do not have this dexterity.

Even to perform the simplest act of drawing or writing requires control of motor activities involving almost the total musculature of the body.

For a child to be able to draw a square, he must, first, be able to maintain an appropriate sitting position, hold his head erect, be able to coordinate the movements of his fingers, hands, wrists, arms. He must have the sense of *laterality,* be able to distinguish between his left side and right, and control the two sides of his body separately and simultaneously.

He must also have the sense of *directionality,* a perception about the coordinates of space, which allows him to project his right-left, up-down orientations. He must also know how to stop his movements—on cue. To do it all, he must have *ocular* as well as *manual* control.

If it takes that much perceptual-motor development just to draw a square, it is obvious that a much greater and broader basic development is required for a child to cope with the full range of academic challenges.

Self-Image and Drive

This analysis of the abilities needed to draw a square, valid in itself, lists only part of the improvements which perceptual-motor training can bring to a child's academic performance. It explains what this training does for the child's perception and motor skills—but not what it does for him emotionally and *psychologically.*

Perceptual-motor training—conducted in an orderly structured way, in an atmosphere where there is no pressure on the child, where work is made to seem like play, where the youngster is always entered into activities where he will encounter some success, and where his achievements are given sincere praise—can have a wonderful effect on a child's self-image, and in turn, on his *drive to learn.*

Many a youngster with below-average academic achievement has been transformed to an achieving student, as a consequence of perceptual-motor training which caused his "I can't" approach to life, born of a succession of failures, to give way to an exuberant and confident *"I can!"* John Tynes, who has witnessed this transformation in the lives of hundreds of young people, puts it this way:

"Many, perhaps most, of the youngsters with learning problems have experienced little but failure since they began school. One failure—in math, reading, writing, whatever—has followed another. Soon failure becomes a pattern. Something must break the pattern, by giving the child a success that is to him tangible and important. We can do it with perceptual-motor training. Over the past three years we have worked with almost every type of handicap, and we have seen again and again how they start to give way as the perceptual-motor program, conducted with strict discipline but with real personal concern and appreciation for the child, gives him a real success, and thus boosts his self-image. After that, the child tends to be happier and more confident; he tries harder, not only in the exercise program but in his studies. And the results show academically."

A Physiological Explanation

Other specialists, particularly neurological researchers, are apt to offer a more physiological explanation of how perceptual-motor training works, how it helps upgrade the child's scholastic performance. They observe that communication between brain and tissues (including muscles) is a two-way proposition: the brain communicates to the muscles through the motor or efferent nerve channels, and the muscles communicate to the brain through the sensory or afferent channels.

The neurological view is that regular repetition of rhythmic, coordination-requiring exercises (i.e., perceptual-motor training), sends sensory nerve messages to the brain area that governs these movements, ultimately causing actual physical changes in the neurological structure—building up brain circuits that permit various physical and mental feats that previously may have been impossible.

Regardless of which explanation (perceptual-motor, psychological or neurological) is accepted, there is no doubt that this type of training *works*. A study conducted at the Shoreline Schools in Seattle, Washington, involved 151 first grade boys and girls in an eight-month test. It found that average youngsters who were given perceptual-motor skill exercises twenty minutes a day, instead of their regular physical education activity, finished the program with a 2.60 grade level reading score, almost five months ahead of the control group.

Other reports have demonstrated the ability of neuromuscular exercise to improve the mental and physical abilities of severely handicapped children, including some who could not walk or talk, lifting many to average and some to above-average performance.

Results of Placentia Program

But there is particularly impressive evidence of the effectiveness of the type of perceptual-motor training program presented by Health and Education Services Corp. (described in this Teacher's Guide) based on the program conducted by John Tynes in the Unified School District of Placentia, California.

Educators all across the country have seen television and radio reports, motion pictures and newspaper stories devoted to the Placentia program. Elementary, high school and college teachers, physicians, psychologists, and representatives of government have reviewed this program. Why has it drawn so much attention?

First, the Placentia program is big—one of the largest such programs ever conducted. It involves nine schools, more than 50 volunteers, over 300 teachers, many hundreds of parents. Approximately a thousand students participate in the program every week, and more than 7,000 have been in it in just three years.

Even before formal research was undertaken, it was obvious to teachers, parents and observers that the Placentia program was producing results—improving bodily coordination, increasing listening skills, stepping up the drive and confidence for learning in hundreds of slow learners.

It was equally apparent that the program was helping non-achievers make real improvements in reading, writing and mathematics—with the elimination of reversals and other learning problems that affect not only the "three R's" but such subjects as art and music. In one school alone, grades improved for 20 of the 28 students in the program.

Then a formal study was made under a program of the Elementary and Secondary Education Act (E.S.E.A. TITLE I), in cooperation with the Evaluation Unit of the California State Department of Education, to measure the effects of the Placentia perceptual-motor training activity on children in this program compared to those experiencing conventional recreation and exercise.

The results were conclusive: *the Placentia perceptual-motor program proved highly effective in improving children's mental and physical abilities. Children in the program advanced in reading skills at one-and-a-half to almost twice the rate of the control group. And 95% of the children with perceptual and coordination problems showed growth as measured by two widely-accepted tests.*

The project extended throughout the 1968–69 school year, from September, 1968, to June, 1969, and involved 150 children—90 with reading problems and 60 with perceptual and motor problems—who took part in the perceptual-motor training; and control groups which engaged in the conventional school exercise and recreation programs. The children came from all five elementary schools in the Placentia District. The project measured the academic ability (indicated by reading skill) and physical ability (shown in strength, coordination and motor skill) of both the TITLE I children and the control group upon the child's entrance into the program, and upon completion. Formal tests were supplemented by teacher and specialist evaluations.

Evaluating the gain in reading skill per month for the control group by the figure 1, the special group receiving John Tynes perceptual-motor training advanced at a rate of 1.6 by the Jastak Test and 1.8 by the Gillmore— i.e., one-and-a-half to almost twice the rate of the comparison group.

The TITLE I study also evaluated sixty target children who tested as having perceptual problems. Comparison of the September Pre-Test and May Post-Test showed that the numbers of children in the "low" and "low average" perceptual skills categories greatly diminished, while those in the "average" and "high" groupings substantially increased.

The control group contained 30 children who took part only in conventional exercise. Their perceptual-motor progress was much less. The number testing "low" in perceptual-motor skills was reduced only slightly; the number testing "low average" was hardly reduced at all.

Most important, 95% (57 out of 60 children) in the Tynes perceptual-motor training program showed some growth on both the Winterhaven and Frostig Tests. The report added, *"All* students showed some growth in motor skills and self-confidence."

Daily school experience at Placentia continues to confirm the test results. Tynes constantly hears from teachers of handicapped and problem students, "They are doing better, now they will try." "Their attention span is better." "They have quit mirror writing." "They are now talking." Even the speech therapists trace improvements to the perceptual-motor training. Many children seem to be far happier. And many boys who before could not go out for sports are now participating in swimming, football and baseball.

John Tynes sums it up when he says, "Almost always, the teachers working with the children in the classroom find that the youngsters who have gone through our program are better able to learn than they were before they came to us."

An equipment package for this training program and guide is available from the Health and Education Services Corporation mentioned above.

John Tynes stresses the importance of using music, reading, and the specialized form of physical education *as a fused part* of the academic curriculum.

Bryant J. Cratty (1971), Ed.D., Professor and Director of the Perceptual Motor Learning Laboratory, UCLA, puts it this way:

"Academic operations have been demonstrated to be improvable through movement experiences, only when the operations (i.e. spelling, letter recognition, reading, etc.) are combined in direct ways with the games and movement tasks presented to the children."

If neglected, this vital bridge between movement and learning process will cause the motor skills to fail in their intended purpose. Dr. Cratty (1971) urges those using such programs to scrutinize their procedures to determine their true efficacy. The books, *Perceptual-Motor Efficiency in Children* (Cratty and Martin 1969), *Active Learning* (Cratty 1971), and *Physical Expression of Intelligence* (Cratty 1972) describe the types of learning games that are an effective bridge. Dr. Cratty (1971) raises the question concerning the effect these movements might have on the later academic performance of pre-school children. No study to date has been done.

This raises another question: Are there certain basic exercises or movements that need to be learned first without any bridge or fusing with the academics? Logic would answer yes.

Take, for an analogy, any sport—football, for example. The basic movements (simple to complex) come first. They are always an essential part of the game. But they themselves are not the game. If one could, by himself, learn well the motions and actions of a football player he still would not be considered a player until he could be properly used with a team on the field.

There is a point where the basics reach a dead end, but this is avoided by integrating, incorporating and fusing them into the total complex of the game. Complexity is built up from simplicity and is always dependent upon it. Any good coach will always stress and insist upon the continual review and practice of the basic fundamentals. A player has first to get into good physical condition before that first scrimmage or he is in for a setback. If a child doesn't have good perceptual-motor development it is likely that he will fail rather than succeed at an academic task.

The point at which a developing maturing movement needs a bridge to the school learning process is not known. This area needs further research. A second-grade child who has the perceptual-motor ability equal to a pre-school four-year-old certainly would need basic training—probably without any bridge. When development reaches the kindergarten level one could assume the need for appropriate bridges to academic learning.

John Tynes relates the incidence of trying to teach seventy-four EMR (Educable Mentally Retarded) students how to swim. He succeeded only with two. Then he took those same students through his perceptual-motor training program. On the second attempt to teach them to swim all but one learned this rewarding skill. What a boost for the youngsters and their parents!

The perceptual-motor training program requires helpers to guide and instruct the children. One year John Tynes recruited the help of eighteen high school pupils who were only one step away from dropping out. The thought that they could be useful and actually see for themselves that what they were accomplishing was of benefit to others became quite a lift to the discouraged pupils. The motivation resulting from this self-concept building was great enough to get at least six of the "helpers" back to their studies. Instead of dropping out, they went on to college and became teachers.

The figure of 33 and 1/3 per cent is a good salvage rate! Mr. Tynes' high schoolers discovered in a very practical way that one of the most self-satisfying endeavors in life is to be a help, blessing and encouragement to someone else.

BIBLIOGRAPHY FOR CHAPTER FIFTEEN

Barsch, Ray H. *Achieving Perceptual-Motor Efficiency.* Special Child Publications, Seattle, 1967

Cratty, Bryant J., *Human Behavior: Exploring Educational Processes,* chapter 10, pp. 204, The University Press, 1971.
Ibid., pp. 191-192.

Cratty, Bryant J., and **Martin,** Sister Margaret Mary, *Perceptual-Motor Efficiency in Children,* Lea & Febiger, 1969, Philadelphia, Penna., 1969.

Cratty, Bryant J., *Active Learning: Games to Enhance Academic Abilities,* Prentice-Hall Inc., Englewood Cliffs, New Jersey, 1971.

Cratty, Bryant J., *Physical Expression of Intelligence,* Prentice-Hall Inc., Englewood Cliffs, New Jersey, 1972.

Frostig, Marianne and **Horne,** David, *The Frostig Program for the Development of Visual Perception,* Teacher's Guide, Follett Pub. Co., Chicago, 1940.

Getman, G. N., et. al. *The Physiology of Readiness,* Minneapolis: Programs to Accelerate School Success, 1964.

Gregory, R.L., *Eye and Brain, the Psychology of Seeing,* World University Library, chapter 11, pp. 209-211, McGraw-Hill Book Co., New York, 1966.

Kephart, Newell C., *The Slow Learner in the Classroom,* Charles E. Merrill Books, Inc., Columbus, Ohio, 1960.

Radler, D. H. and **Kephart,** Newell C., *Success Through Play,* Harper and Row Publishers, New York, 1960.

Teacher's Guide: Perceptual-Motor Training Program, Introduction: Perceptual-Motor Training in Theory and Practice, pp. 5-11, Health and Education Services Corporation, Bensenville, Ill., 1971.

Tynes, John, This Is a Program that Works, *Teacher's Guide: Perceptual-Motor Training Program,* chapter 1, pp. 2-3, Health and Education Services Corporation, Bensenville, Ill., 1971.

CHAPTER SIXTEEN

SPEECH AND APHASIC PROBLEMS

Man's ability to communicate with a spoken and written language makes him unique among living things. These communication skills provide satisfying fulfillment in all his social relationships.

A lag in the proper development of language severely handicaps an otherwise normal person. The loss—partial or complete—of an ability to communicate verbally is called "aphasia."

The term "aphasia" is limited by some to a disorder affecting the comprehension and use of language at the central integrative level of symbolic formulation (Wepman and Jones 1966). This means that once the brain has received information it is unable either to understand, comprehend or use the information properly by itself or in association with other information. Problems of input to, or reception by, the brain Dr. Wepman calls the "sensory agnosias," of which there are 12 types. Problems of output from, or expression by, the brain, are called "motor apraxias" of which there are seven types. With a total auditory agnosia the person is deaf. With total verbal apraxia the person is mute.

In the sensory problems the auditory and visual stimuli are being properly received by the brain, only to be misinterpreted. It is not a question of locating a problem with the auditory acuity of the ear, nor the visual acuity of the eye.

Others classify language problems as "receptive aphasia" or "expressive aphasia," or a combination of both.

Speech problems can be divided as follows:

1 Articulation disorders—speech sounds are not correctly used.
2 Voice disorders—phonation is incorrectly used.
3 Rhythm disorders—sounds, words and sentences do not flow correctly so that a person may stutter, stammer or clutter.
4 Language disorders—the usage of vocabulary, grammar and thought processes are incorrect.

An example of the last named disorder is delayed speech in a child. The youngster says his first words or first short sentences later in life than is expected of him.

Problems of Aphasia

Wepman and Jones (1966) use a psycholinguistic process through which they distinguish five types of aphasia. These categories correspond to the stages a child reaches in his development of a proper language. Or they represent the various levels to which one may regress from full, normal speech patterns following injury to the speech areas of the brain resulting from a stroke or an accident or other disease conditions. Recovery can be charted back up through the types or levels progressing from the maximum point of regression.

The degree of recovery is affected by several variables such as the age of the patient, the extent of the injury, the involvement of the professional staff, the family concern and other factors.

Five Types of Aphasia

1 Syntactic

Loss or misuse of grammatical form. In severe cases, speech will be telegraphic in nature; i.e., "Daughter . . . home . . . Monday," for "My daughter will be home on Monday."

In less severe cases, the final /s/ morpheme, /ing/ or /ed/ endings, or other inflected grammatical forms may be dropped or added inappropriately; i.e., "He put on his pair of shoe." "He added a boating to his collection."

2 Semantic

Inability or difficulty in substantive word selection. In severe cases nouns or other substantive words may be omitted, or a pronoun substituted. In less severe cases, substantive words inappropriate to meaning may be supplied. In least severe cases, words in the same meaning category may be substituted; i.e., "See the thing in my hand" (where the pronoun "thing" substitutes for "pencil"); "See the house in my hand" (where "house" substitutes for "pencil"); "See the pen in my hand" (where "pen" substitutes for "pencil").

3 Pragmatic

Where many words are present of both syntactic and semantic classes but are inappropriately used. Many semantic words are substituted for by neologisms. Meaning is lost because of the inappropriateness of the verbal expression; i.e., "That man is clipping the kreples."

4 Jargon

Where intelligibility is lost because the verbal utterance is unintelligible. All of the phonemes seem to be present, but they are rarely produced in understandable morphemic clusters; i.e., "te da de mo ah too" (spoken with adequate speech inflection as though telling an intelligible something to the listener).

5 Global
Literally no verbal effort beyond an automatic expression or two.

Here is a startling fact that might be upsetting to some professionals. Unfortunately, some, hearing it for the first time are suspicious. But don't most of us react apprehensively to new things that our training and our experience hasn't taught us? Later we find out after careful investigation that quite a few new things are valid and make sense.

This is the statement: Not all speech problems are psychological in origin, excluding those caused by disease or injury. Neurological factors also play a part, in addition to the psychological causes, in causing stuttering, stammering, or cluttering. Anyone with a speech problem resulting from neurological dysfunction is certain to have obvious emotional repercussions because this important and unique human achievement is not fully developed. This inability is a serious blow to the sufferer's ego and self esteem. It leaves the psyche severely shaken. The aphasic knows he's different because he can't speak like others.

The nature of electrically induced speech disturbance is outlined and discussed in a study on speech by Dean E. Wooldridge (1963). The author describes the work of Dr. Penfield and his associates as they recreated various aphasic patterns by the electrical stimulation of any of the three speech areas of the cortex of the brain which they outlined over their years of study.

Is it too illogical to suppose that when the brain itself discharges an abnormal amount of electricity, charted by an abnormal EEG which reveals a paroxysmal burst or a spike type discharge in a speech area, that such could be the basis of an aphasic problem on a neurological basis?

The EEG is not all that specific, of course, when taken with the full skull cap in place. But the implications should signal the need for further investigation along these lines.

In 1971 the author was privileged to serve on one of the diagnostic teams for the Los Angeles County Superintendent of Schools Aphasia Program. Our observations showed that children with this handicap in varying degrees of receptive expressive aphasia problems did much more poorly on the neurological examination as compared with the EH (educationally handicapped) children of the same age. (See the comparative table in Chapter 8, pages 58, 59). Most of them, therefore, fit the diagnosis of the typical hyperkinetic but were more severely effected and had in addition, aphasia—their main problem.

Testing the aphasic child requires involved procedures in three basic steps:

1   The examination team must be larger because the specialists need the usual psychological and neurological workup but in addition a speech pathologist or therapist must make a detailed analysis of the child's verbal communication abilities and deficits.

2   Testing these children takes more time, ingenuity, and patience because of their basic communication problem.

3   Special attention must be given to the selection of tests. Some young patients were thought to be retarded by teachers in regular schools only because a verbal IQ test, such as the Stanford Binet, is most inappropriate for a school-aged child who has a vocabulary of only 50 words or for one whose speech is jargon (Wepman classification type number four).

On the other hand, when a totally non-verbal performance IQ test like the Leiter exam was given a surprising number of these children had a normal IQ. A few children had scores showing IQs characteristic of bright and superior ranges. By the same token, even the performance portion of the WISC IQ test could give an inaccurate low result because verbal instructions are included in portions of that test. The Stanford-Binet and WISC examinations are appropriate for the milder types of aphasic problems.

Following are listed some of the tests employed by the diagnostic team:

IQ	PERCEPTION
Leiter	Bender-Gestalt
Stanford-Binet	Geometric Designs
Wechsler Intelligence	Drawings:
Scale for Children (WISC)	House-Tree-Person (H-T-P)
	Draw a Person (D-A-P)

LANGUAGE

Illinois Test of Psycholinguistic Ability (ITPA)
Assessment of Children Language Comprehension (ACLC)
Northwestern Syntax (Laura Lee)
Berry-Talbott Language Tests
Wepman Auditory Discrimination Test

ACHIEVEMENT

Wide Range Achievement Tests (WRAT)
Appropriate for 2nd grade and higher
  • reading
  • spelling
  • arithmetic
Survey of Primary Reading Development (SPRD)
  Appropriate up to 4th grade

NEUROLOGICAL

Neurological exam used for the EH pupil
  If unable to perform the above then the Clark Motor
  Development Scale for Children
Electroencephalogram (EEG)

Testing is important, but so is the background history of the child. This takes into consideration social, emotional, medical and other data that might be extraordinary. The examiner should note carefully whether the child experienced any severe emotional-physical trauma or excessive rejection or isolation that would deprive him of adequate verbal communication contacts. These could cause aphasia on an emotional withdrawal basis.

Severe trauma and rejection can dramatically cause aphasia, as the true story of an unfortunate girl named Laura illustrates.

At twelve, Laura was hideously deformed, withdrawn and strangely mute. She was diagnosed as schizophrenic, the unwanted child of alcoholic parents.

The youngster came to the attention of the world at 18 months when she was treated in a Brooklyn hospital following a beating by her parents. Her mother and father both beat the child in alcohol-induced rages, pummeling her with their fists and flailing her with straps that caused welts the size of raisins. Only shrieks and moans came from the little girl's crib, angering her parents even further.

Neighbors one evening detected in Laura's cry more animality than before so they summoned police who crashed into the apartment. Following the plaintive wails they rushed to the kitchen where Laura was being burned alive in a large frying pan by her merciless parents.

Hospital physicians nursed the infant's body back to life. Her mind was not so easily restored. For many days she rarely moved, ate poorly, refused play objects and sat for hours on the floor staring mutely.

At three, Laura was still hospitalized. Her eyes were crossed, the veins of her legs varicosed, and her spine bent into a curve.

At five Laura still had not pronounced one word. Doctors labeled her mentally deficient; others saw symptoms of withdrawal characteristic of schizophrenia.

Just as officials were deciding to sentence the child to a state mental hospital a group of Catholic sisters by chance had room for her. For seven years they nursed her in a true "home," but Laura said nothing, numbly withdrawn from the real world.

By chance a young psychiatrist asked for the privilege of working with Laura. In periodic sessions that stretched into years he coaxed the child to respond. Only an occasional tear from Laura's eyes rewarded his efforts. Then suddenly one day Laura accepted a candy bar and promptly retreated quickly back into her emotional dream world of fantasy. Another day when a group of raucous boys on roller skates breezed past Laura grabbed for the doctor's waist. *She is not psychotic after all!* reasoned the psychiatrist.

When his patient went back into silence the psychiatrist built a miniature house where a toy family lived. He moved the characters around, staging a fight finally between the parents that ended in a beating for the baby.

"No, no, no!" screamed Laura, struggling out of her chair. Her body quivered with a decade and a half of suppressed rage at the scene. For the doctor, that scream was the greatest single sound he had ever heard.

Surgical procedures repaired her spine and her legs. The emotional block released by her scream, her speech improved measurably. She entered classes at a nearby school and with impressive catch-up skills she soon became much like the other teen-agers in the home. When her parents were released from the mental hospital and returned to see her, Laura rejected them completely.

Dr. Richard D'Ambrosio, practicing psychoanalyst in Brooklyn, was the patient specialist who brought Laura from a living death to a near normal life. He tells her story in his book, *No Language But a Cry.*

At 18, Laura left the home and the care of D'Ambrosio. She was a high school graduate and her body and mind today are nearly normal. She afterward received training as a baby nurse and took a job caring for young children.

Whenever a specific cause can be found for an existing malady which occurs only infrequently the case can be used as a guide to selecting the main type of therapy to be pursued, as in the severe case of Laura's experience illustrated above.

Testing by the diagnostic team revealed another possible error regarding some of the aphasic children sent for evaluation who previously were diagnosed as "autistic" (childhood schizophrenia or pre-schizoid). Their behavior added to their lack of greatly reduced speech would lead one to believe these diagnoses until the full testing was completed.

Then the big question arises: "Are these children truly autistic because of an emotional-psychiatric problem caused by the environment and/or a genetic-hereditary process? Or is there apparent lack of proper contact and response to the world of reality about them due to the fact that their senses of visual, auditory and tactile perception, or their ability to integrate these various types of perceptual stimuli received in the brain, or their faculty for oral or written language expression are malfunctioning so poorly that they are indeed "out of contact"?

In most of the cases recorded the diagnosis showed one or a combination of the latter causes contributed to the problem. The neurological physical-perceptual-motor dysfunction of their brains were keeping their minds from having a proper physical contact with the world around them. Such degrees of neurological dysfunction provided emotional frustration, anxiety and acting out through bizarre behavior in a hurry.

These opposing views on schizophrenia in children are discussed in the article "Perceptual and Perceptual-Motor Dissociation" (Birch and Walker 1966).

Perceptual disabilities rather than emotional disturbances, according to Bryson (1972), may be the main problem contributing to the production of bizarre behavior patterns in autistic children.

How would you react if you understood all the information your senses sent you from your environment yet you could not speak or had only the use of a relatively few words? Try functioning just for a day without saying a word in a learning situation and see how your emotions are affected. You will better understand afterward the aphasic's behavior.

The results of clinical studies further support the neurological basis of some speech problems. One double-blind study (Gilbreath 1969) of 12 children who stuttered showed that Dilantin® proved helpful in 10 of them. Five showed dramatic improvement; four showed modest improvement and one showed a small measure of improvement.

In a second study by Bowling (1965) of 14 stutterers with normal intelligence using d-amphetamine, 12 improved at the .01 level of significance. Improvement ranged from 7.4 per cent to 85.6 per cent, with the median of 20.5 per cent. These stutterers also experienced the same paradoxical reverse effect that the hyperactive patient receives from this type of medication as it calms the physical concomitants associated with stuttering.

A third study—this one carried out by Fish and Bowling (1962)—was made on 28 mentally retarded patients. Fourteen showed improvement when placed on d-amphetamine sulphate (Dexedrine®). Eight of the remaining 14 showed improvement when they were placed on trifluoperazine (Stelazine®).

A fourth study (Fish and Bowling 1962) of 106 mentally retarded patients with various types of speech defects were arranged in a double blind study using dextro-amphetamine sulphate and a placebo. The stutterers were the only ones who showed definite improvement as compared with the placebo group. Three who were long-term severe stutterers had such a dramatic improvement that a change took place that involved the whole course of their lives!

A study utilizing dextro-amphetamine sulfate reports positive results in eight out of fourteen cases—six of them improved 20 per cent to 80 per cent in four weeks. The small sample, lack of control group and the short follow-up study limits its usefulness (Riley, Bowling, Fish 1965).

Three additional studies with stutterers representing 37 (Bente and Schonharl, E., and Krump-Erlangen, J., 1956), 140 (Sack 1968), and 24 (Schonharl 1960) patients respectively report beneficial effects from using medicine of the hydantoin type. Diphenylhydantoin (Dilantin®) is specifically mentioned in the third report.

The use of such medications as thioridazine (Mellaril®) and amphetamine sulfate (Benzedrine®) is mentioned in an abstract dealing with cluttering. These medications offer temporary improvement. The subjects involved had abnormal EEGs and several of the same cardinal symptoms of the hyperkinetic patient (Weiss 1968).

The author has had several children as private patients who were typical hyperactives who also stuttered and for whom medication was effective in either fully or partially removing the problem. In addition to the medications already mentioned, methylphenidate HCL (Ritalin®) should be added to the list.

In addition, there has been a few patients whose pronunciation problems were improved with medication prescribed primarily for their hyperactive learning disability because both Glyndon Riley, Ph.D., Speech Pathologist, and the author have seen its effectiveness in private practice. Perhaps the speech problem isn't helped directly by the medication. But at least the speech therapist and the special classes teacher can work better with the child after he is calm, more attentive and less distracted.

A speech or aphasic disorder should have a thorough work up, including language, psychological, social and neurological diagnostic measures. The therapy program should include treatment from each area as indicated. Further research is in order and is needed to clarify more specifically the use of medication in these areas.

Ponder this question: If the neurologically impaired EH and EMR student can be helped by coordinative development and perceptual-motor training exercises then it should be logical to assume that the neurologically impaired speech or aphasic pupil should respond as rewardingly. The greater neurological involvement of both would indicate the need for either a more intense or a longer program.

The greater the problem, the greater the need for steady, consistent, patient, longer-range, thorough programs of remediation. What a joy it is to see handicapped children receive help and to watch them respond—whether the response be little or much. There are many children with moderate to severe learning disabilities who urgently need help but who are not finding it.

Let us continue to meet the challenge presented. Our rewards will be great as young lives reach their full potential and then in turn serve others in need.

BIBLIOGRAPHY FOR CHAPTER SIXTEEN

Bente, D., **Schonharl,** E., and **Krump-Erlangen,** J., Electroencephalographic findings in stutterers and their application to medical therapy (in German), *Archiv fur Ohren-,* Nasen-and Kehlkopfheilkunde, 169: 513-519, 1956.

Birch, Herbert G., and **Walker,** Harry A., Perceptual and Perceptual-Motor Dissociation, *Archives of General Psychiatry,* Vol. 14, pp. 113-118, Feb., 1966.

Bowling, Evelyn Burge, Speech and Hearing Therapist, Fairview State Hospital, Costa Mesa, California, Research paper at California State College at Fullerton, June 10, 1965.

Bryson, Carolyn Q., Short Term Memory and Cross-Modal Information Processing in Autistic Children, *Journal of Learning Disabilities,* Vol. 5, No. 2, pp. 81-91, Feb., 1972.

Fish, Charles H., and **Bowling,** Evelyn, The Effect of D-Amphetamine and a tranquilizing agent, Trifluoperazine on stutterers, Fairview State Hospital, Costa Mesa, California, October and November, 1962.

Fish, Charles H., and **Bowling,** Evelyn, Effect of Amphetamines on Speech Defects in the Mentally Retarded, *California Medicine,* Vol. 96, pp. 109-111, published by the California Medical Association, Feb., 1962.

Gilbreath, Mrs. Jeanne, The Use of the Drug Dilantin as an Adjunct to Therapy with Children Who Stutter, a paper presented at the California Speech and Hearing Association Conference, San Francisco, March, 1969.

Riley, Glyndon, D., **Bowling,** Evelyn, and **Fish,** Charles H., The Effect of Dextroamphetamine on Stuttering in Individuals with Normal Intelligence, paper presented at the American Speech and Hearing Association (ASHA) Convention, Chicago, Nov., 1965.

Sack, L., The Effects of Sodium Dilantin on Stuttering Behavior, University of California, Los Angeles, Doctoral Thesis, 1968.

Schonharl, E., Pharmacotherapeutic experiences in speech and vocal disturbances (in German), *Med. Exp.,* 2: 179-183, 1960.

Weiss, Deso A., Abstract: Cluttering, an Imbalance of Central Language, *Modern Medicine,* Feb. 10, 1969, p. 181. Original Article: Cluttering, *Pediatric Clinics of North America,* Vol. 15, pp. 705-720, 1968.

Wepman, Joseph M., and **Jones,** Lyle V., Aphasia: Diagnostic Description and Therapy, pp. 127-128, *Proceedings of Conference on Research Needs in Rehabilitation of Patients with Stroke,* January 19-20, 1966. *Ibid.,* pp. 129-133.

Wooldridge, Dean E., Personality and Speech, *The Machinery of the Brain,* chapter 8, pp. 153-165, McGraw-Hill Book Co., New York, 1963.

CHAPTER SEVENTEEN

FOOD AND ITS 'VICTIMS'

Most people like to eat. We Americans should be thankful both for an abundance of food and for a great variety of tasty nourishment. Nevertheless, some of us are too poor to be properly nourished and others are malnourished because of poor eating habits. The availability of adequate quantities of good food does not guarantee proper nutrition for all citizens.

Families in North America were wealthier in 1965 than they were 10 years earlier, yet there were more families with poor diets in 1965 than in the decade before. This startling fact was revealed by the U.S. Department of Agriculture Food Consumption Survey in a published report which showed that only 50 per cent of the families surveyed in 1965 had "good" diets, compared to 60 per cent in 1955. The percentage of families with "poor" diets rose from 15 per cent in 1955 to 20 per cent in 1965 (Wenck 1968).

As might be expected, the higher the family income and the greater the expenditure for food, the better the quality of the diet. However, only two-thirds of the high income families had good diets and nine per cent had poor diets.

The 10 per cent decrease in good nutrition within the short span of 10 years should give us all great concern. In one decade the number of "good" diets (providing sufficient amounts of all nutrients needed for good health) decreased and the number of "poor" diets (seriously lacking in several nutrients) increased. Nutrients most often found lacking were calcium, vitamin A and vitamin C (Wenck 1970).

The reasons for this trend toward poorer diets can be found in changes in eating habits revealed in surveys by nutrition experts. Does the following sound familiar?

Bruce gets up for school, dresses, gulps a glass of milk and dashes out the door. On the way to the bus stop he finishes a candy bar he had in his pocket, left over from the day before.

At noon he eats a hamburger for lunch with some potato chips and some cookies. After school he nibbles on a handful or two of a sugar-coated cereal. Just before supper he eats a doughnut despite his mother's plea, "Can't you wait?"

"But gee, Mom, I'm hungry!" he complains.

At supper a balanced meal has been prepared and "picky" eater Bruce consumes what he likes and therefore does not reward his body with a balanced meal. After supper while watching TV he snacks on a soft drink with some candy coated popcorn.

Bruce is hyperactive and needs more fuel, but his poor eating habits are leaving him malnourished. He is filling his stomach on popular snack foods which are really "junk" foods because they supply mostly calories for energy but little nutrition essential for body building and repair.

How to Nibble Nourishingly

The secret of proper snacking is to *go easy on junk*—soft drinks, popsicles, fruit drinks, punch, candy, potatoes, corn chips, cookies, doughnuts, sugared cereals, sugar-coated popcorn (Wenck 1970).

FOUNDATION DIET

The foundation diet will provide approximately 1200 calories.

Milk Group	1 glass = 8 ounces Equivalents— 1 oz. American Cheese = ¾ glass milk ½ cup creamed cottage cheese = ⅓ glass milk ½ cup ice cream = ¼ glass milk
Meat Group	1 serving = 2–3 ounces cooked Equivalents for 1 ounce protein 1 oz. American or Swiss Cheese 1 oz. Luncheon meat 2 tablespoons peanut butter ½ cup cooked dried beans or peas
Vegetables	1 serving = ½ cup cooked 1 cup raw
Bread	1 serving = 1 slice bread* ¾ cup dry cereal* ½ cup cooked cereal* *Restored, whole grain or enriched

This is the foundation for a good diet.
Use more of these and other foods as needed
for growth, for activity, and for desirable weight.

Used by permission: National Dairy Council of America.

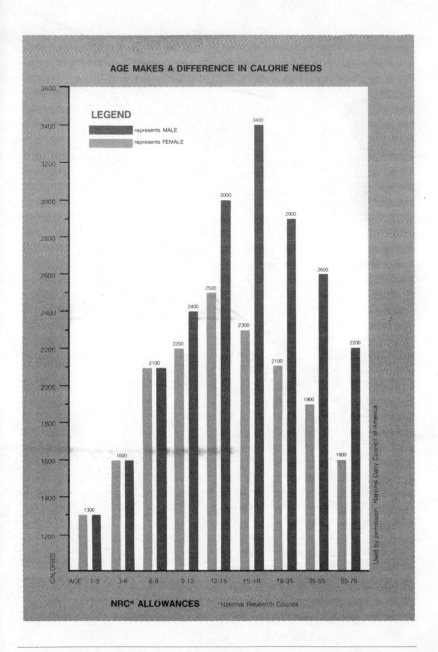

AGE MAKES A DIFFERENCE IN CALORIE NEEDS

Choose foods from the same four food groups that should characterize your meals:

I   THE MILK GROUP

Milk, buttermilk, chocolate milk, cocoa
"Double" milk or "instant breakfast"
Eggnog, shakes, malts, peanut butter milk
Ice cream, pudding, custard, yogurt
Cheese—cottage, cheddar, brick, etc.
Cheese spread, cottage cheese dip

II   THE MEAT (PROTEIN) GROUP

Peanuts and other nuts, peanut butter
Hard cooked or deviled eggs
Luncheon meat, sausage, liver sausage
Dried beef, jerky, sunflower seeds
Canned tuna, "fish 'n chips," herring
Hot dogs, hamburgers, tacos

III   THE FRUIT AND VEGETABLE GROUP

Raw vegetables such as carrots, celery, cauliflower, cucumber, green
pepper, cabbage, radishes
Pickles, olives
Fresh fruits of all kinds
Dried fruits such as raisins, apricots, prunes (brush teeth afterwards—
sticky sugars can cause tooth decay)
Fruit juice—citrus, tomato—and fruit *juice* drinks
Frozen juice bars made from fruit juice
Combinations such as celery stalks or apple slices spread with cheese
or peanut butter

IV   THE BREAD AND CEREAL GROUP

Crackers (especially those made from enriched flour), wheat wafers
Enriched bread, oven-toasted tortillas
Non-sugared cereals, plain popcorn
Pizza, sandwiches, crackers and cheese
Homemade cookies with oatmeal, nuts, dry milk, raisins,
peanut butter, etc.

A Guide to Good Eating

Use Daily:

Milk Group

3 or more glasses milk—Children smaller glasses for some children under 8

4 or more glasses—Teen-agers

2 or more glasses—Adults

Cheese, ice cream and other milk-made foods can supply part of the milk

Meat Group

2 or more servings

Meats, fish, poultry, eggs, or cheese—with dry beans, peas, nuts as alternates

Vegetables and Fruits

4 or more servings

include dark green or yellow vegetables; citrus fruit or tomatoes

Breads and Cereals

4 or more servings

Enriched or whole grain Added milk improves nutritional values

When mother shops for food

The lady of the house is usually the one who determines what kinds of foods her family members will eat at home. Her choices at the supermarket mold her children's eating habits. Those habits—learned in early years—tend to carry over into adulthood and extend also to away-from-home eating. If mother encourages her children to enjoy nutritious snacks they are less likely to develop a taste for "junk" foods.

To be eaten consistently and therefore to do the most good, snack foods must be convenient, ready-to-eat, fast and fun! For example, few children will stop to clean a carrot. But they will eat carrots if they find them at *eye level* in the refrigerator, all cleaned, cut into strips, crisped in water and ready to munch.

The added bonus of nutritious snack foods is that they are a better buy. *They actually give you more food for your money* than do the "junk" foods. The wise buyer wins two ways—healthwise and moneywise.

Obvious or clinical malnutrition is easy to recognize in a child. The symptoms are diarrhea, listlessness, distended abdomen and slow growth. The classical diagnoses are (1) kwashiorkor, meaning "golden boy," or "red boy" in a West African language. It is a syndrome produced by severe protein deficiency which among other changes results in the unusual dark hair to become first red and later golden. (2) Marasmus is a progressive wasting and emaciation, especially in infants, due to inadequate caloric intake. The term "marasmus" can also be used in referring to infants who waste away and die because of a profound lack of tender, loving care and the human contact, even when an adequate diet is supplied. This type is not under consideration here. (3) Marasmic kwashiorkor is a deficiency in both calories and protein. Hidden or subclinical malnutrition is not easy to detect. The Citizens Board of Inquiry into Hunger and Malnutrition in the United States (1968) published its findings in the book *Hunger U.S.A.,* (Beacon Press), and concluded that each identified case of kwashiorkor (protein-lack), pellagra (niacin or niacinamide lack), scurvy (vitamin C lack), or the like, came from typical cases of malnutrition. These classic cases are just like the tip of the iceberg and point to "a far greater number of borderline cases." Each case registered indicates that many more were hidden and therefore undocumented.

Types of Nutritional Lack

1   Unavailability of food. This is the result of
    a. low income
    b. poor shopping habits

c. missing nutrients because of poor soil, over processing, or over cooking

2 Nutrients in the diet below the normal needs of the eater

3 Poor digestion and/or poor absorption. Adequate supplies of food may be available and the child may eat a balanced diet. But if digestion is not thorough, the incompletely digested particles cannot be absorbed. Such is the case with a child or adult who cannot drink a glass of milk without developing stomach pain, abdominal distention, borboygmi (a growling stomach) and diarrhea. This malady is caused by the deficiency in the digestive system of an enzyme called lactase which digests the sugar found in milk which is called lactose. Because it cannot be digested and changed into another form of sugar such as glucose it cannot be absorbed. By remaining in the digestive system it produces the problems mentioned above (Sleisenger, Weser, Bayless, Rosensweig, Huang, Simoons, and McCracken 1971).

There are other digestive system deficiencies which can prevent digestion and absorption of needed nutrients. Specific relationships of these deficiencies to brain dysfunction and learning disabilities has not been established. Nevertheless, it would logically follow that the new interest in clinical nutrition might well show some pertinent connections.

4 Normal amounts of nutrients inadequate for *above normal* needs. To explain this in detail, here is an excerpt* from a book by Dr. Linus Pauling (1970):

The molecules of many enzymes consist of two parts: the pure protein part, called the apoenzyme, and a non-protein part, called the coenzyme. The active enzyme, called the holoenzyme, is the apoenzyme with the coenzyme attached to it. Often the coenzyme is a vitamin molecule or a closely related molecule. It is known, for example, that a number of different enzymes in the human body, catalyzing different chemical reactions, have thiamine pyrophosphate, a derivative of thiamine (vitamin B_1), as coenzyme.

In some cases of genetic disease the enzyme is not absent, but is present with diminished activity. One way in which the defective gene can operate is to produce an apoenzyme with abnormal structure, such that it

*Used by permission:

From *Vitamin C and the Common Cold* by Linus Pauling. W. H. Freeman and Co., Copyright © 1970.

FOOD AND ITS VICTIMS

does not combine readily with the coenzyme to form the active enzyme. Under ordinary physiological conditions, with the normal concentration of coenzyme, perhaps only one per cent of the abnormal apoenzyme has combined with the coenzyme. According to the principles of chemical equilibrium, a larger fraction of the abnormal apoenzyme could be made to combine with the coenzyme by increasing the concentration of the coenzyme in the body fluids. If the concentration were to be increased one hundred times, most of the apoenzyme molecules might combine with the coenzyme, to give essentially the normal amount of active enzyme.

There is accordingly the possibility that the disease could be kept under control by the ingestion by the patient of a very large amount of the vitamin that serves as a coenzyme. This sort of orthomolecular therapy, involving only a substance normally present in the human body (the vitamin), is, in my opinion, the preferable therapy.

An example of a disease that might be controlled in this way is the disease methylmalonicaciduria. The patients with this disease are deficient in the active enzyme that catalyzes the conversion of a simple substance, methylmalonic acid, to succinic acid. It is known that cyanocobalamin (vitamin B_{12}) serves as the coenzyme for this reaction. It is found that the provision of very large amounts of vitamin B_{12}, giving concentrations about a thousand times the normal concentration, causes the reaction to proceed at the normal rate for many of the patients.

Above-normal needs could result from many causes, as follows:

a. Hyperkinesis (overactivity in children or adults). The food intake of an overactive child is usually quite above normal. He is most apt to require excessive carbohydrates, starches and sweets. Usually such a child is thin. Many such children, when placed on appropriate medication, ironically slow down to a normal speed, eat less but begin to gain weight. The fuel requirements for all their cells have been reduced.

b. Higher cell wall threshold. In such a circumstance, the body requires a higher concentration than normal of a substance in the blood stream in order for it to pass through the wall of a cell whose permeability has decreased, thus making it more difficult for substance to go through it into the cell.

c. High metabolic need within the cell. The overactive child or adult burns (metabolizes) more blood sugar (glucose) for fuel. In order to do this the cell needs higher proportionate amounts of other ingredients among which are insulin (a hormone) and thiamine (vitamin B_1). If these are not in the cell in proper amounts the sugar cannot be utilized. Therefore, one would assume that the amounts of thiamine and insulin needed by an overactive child or adult are greater than that needed by the normally active child.

The study of biological functions of components within the cells themselves is called Molecular Biology (Udenfriend 1971). Reference to the hypothesis of a molecular code for the processing of information by the brain whether it be genetic, which is recognized by the scientific world, or acquired, which is under present investigation, involves observations made on the quantitative and qualitative changes in the RNA (ribonucleic acid) of cells involved in learning as well as changes in protein synthesis (Ungar 1971).

This could well mean that if specific nutritional needs, particularly protein, are not met while an individual is forming such cells—in the mother's womb or afterward as their body is building to its peak strength and size—then proper production of RNA cannot take place.

If relatives of the child had similar nutritional lacks, with or without a hereditary tendency to learning problems, then such a genetic-family nutritional lack only reinforces the child's unfortunate chance of not learning adequately.

Nobody would think of putting 90 octane gasoline in a car with a high compression engine requiring 104 octane fuel or above. But inadvertently we often do the very same thing to our precious "high compression" human engines.

Hopefully, further scientific investigation will shed light on these important and greatly neglected aspects of human nutrition.

d. Unknown causes. Mysterious reasons for inadequate nutrition exist. Future investigation will need to uncover them as man searches for more knowledge and wisdom to solve his continuing problems.

Can foods produce bad side effects like medicines?

When Billy took a certain brand of medicine it produced a headache.

When he ate certain types of citrus foods he became very irritable.

Medicine and food can both produce ill effects on the human body. The reactions can be classified as allergy, foreign body reaction, or adverse medicine, drug or chemical reaction. Food is an organic chemical; medicine can be either an organic or an inorganic chemical.

When Billy takes a different kind of medicine of the inorganic type he can settle down in class and learn with no side effects. He can eat numerous foods without any adverse reactions and they are beneficial. This time both medicine and food are helpful. Is there, after all, any difference between them?

A person can be allergic to the foods he eats, to the pollens or other air-borne substances he breathes, or to things that contact our skin. Food allergies are the more common.

Most people think of allergy in terms of hayfever, asthma, poison ivy, poison oak, hives from certain fruits and other obvious manifestations of allergic responses. There are, in addition to the obvious, the more subtle forms of allergy that can effect the central nervous system, particularly the brain, and thus produce learning or behavior problems or both.

Allergy can be cause-related to the following entities of the nervous system: Tension-fatigue syndrome, neurologic and psychic syndrome, headaches, epilepsy, neuropathies and demyelinative diseases and minimal brain dysfunctions in children. Each of these is studied as to possible cause, diagnosis and treatment in a book, *Allergy of the Nervous System* (Speer 1970).

The removal of allergy-producing foods from a diet can reduce the symptoms in some children with minimal brain dysfunction—even to the point of causing improved changes in the EEG (brain wave test) and the IQ, as well as the disappearance of enuresis (bed wetting). Specific tests for allergy to air borne (inhalants), food (ingestants) and skin (contactants) allergens have been formulated (Speer 1970).

Elimination or trial diets work well for determining the culprits in food allergy, rather than skin tests and other laboratory procedures which are inaccurate in attempts to detect food allergens (Speer 1970).

The nine food allergens giving the highest incidence in a survey of 1,000 patients are milk, chocolate, cola, corn, citrus, egg, legumes (peas, beans, etc.), tomatoes, and wheat. Other foods are listed too, and the incidence is divided into three age groups (Speer 1970).

A new syndrome is being observed in young children and a preliminary report has been published in medical literature. Those involved have a family history of allergic symptoms as well as that of a carbohydrate-related metabolic disease like diabetes. The syndrome is characterized by emotional intensity (easily irritated or frustrated), emotional lability (one moment happy and playful, the next out of sorts, whining and crying), motor hyperactivity (overactive), and sleep problems.

In older children the observations noted there were additional problems of defective ego controls so that they would be impulsive and aggressive and suffer learning difficulties. Although the description of these children is quite similar to that of the hyperkinetic learning disabled child described in earlier chapters, treatment consisted of eliminating the following foods from the diet: milk products, eggs, citric acid and chocolate containing foods, nuts, fish, grapes, and whole wheat. Some responded to the diet but those who didn't within six weeks were considered as not having this particular syndrome. A big problem is adhering to the diet (Weirs and Kaufman 1971).

One notices certain distinct similarities between the new syndrome and the children with minimal brain dysfunction outlined in the book, *Allergy of the Nervous System* (Speer 1970).

An otolaryngologist (ear, nose and throat specialist) reports that some cases of dizziness and associated deafness resulted from improper diet. When the offending foods were avoided the symptoms disappeared. The actual condition is called Meniere's disease. It is characterized by vertigo, nausea, nystagmus and hearing loss.

The foods most commonly listed as the cause of ear problems are wheat, corn, eggs, and milk. This condition has multiple causes, but food allergy is one of them (Clemis 1971). This specialist, Jack D. Clemis, M.D., is in the process of perfecting a cytotoxic test for food allergies which could greatly enhance diagnosis and treatment.

Dangerous Diets

Special diets for religious purposes are becoming increasingly popular. The devotees insist they are a means of obtaining a spiritual awakening. The Zen Macrobiotic diets are an example of these excesses.

From a health and nutritional standpoint these diets are certainly dangerous. They are a major contributor to health problems among the zealots employing them. The danger extends not as much to the adults as to their children who are robbed of important body-building vitamins. Such diets can cause scurvy (lack of Vitamin C), anemia, hypoproteinemia (low blood proteins), hypocalcemia (low blood calcium), emaciation due to starvation and other forms of malnutrition.

Restricted fluid intake which accompanies these diets has resulted in loss of kidney function. Some fatalities have been reported (Council on Foods and Nutrition 1971).

Select diets for the treatment of appendicitis, cancer and other diseases not directly associated with nutritional problems are unfounded fads fraught with fatal potential.

Special diets, especially for children, should be under the supervision of specialists who are trained and qualified in the field of nutrition.

There is no substitute for good nutrition resulting from a well balanced diet. If problems persist despite a balanced diet, then the patient should seek professional help to determine what part, if any, nutrition is playing in the condition.

Megavitamin therapy

Both favorable and unfavorable reports have been published in medical literature about Megavitamin Therapy. Among the reports to come out of the current controversy on this subject are some which deal with the hyperactive learning disability child so mention of the phenomenon is made here.

The dosage range of vitamins can be divided into three groups:

1 Regular daily dose, taken simply as a dietary supplement for no specific medical reason other than the maintenance of good health. Typical would be a dosage of vitamin C ranging between 50 and 150 mgm.

2 Therapeutic dose, usually recommended by a physician for patients having a medical need to overcome such things as severe illness or for assisting healing following surgery. Example: the dosage of vitamin C would be 500 mgm.

3 Megavitamin dose, an amount in large proportions which should be taken only under the supervision of a physician. The dosage is enormous. Example: dosage of vitamin C upwards of 3,000 to 4,000 mgm. daily. Note: A woman with sickle cell thalassemia, a type of anemia, was thrown into an anemic crisis by high doses of vitamin C (Goldstein 1971).

When Massive Vitamin Doses Help

Articles in medical journals today are not in agreement on the question of administering megavitamins to children who are autistic, pre-schizophrenic, schizophrenic, hyperactive and who have learning disabilities. Much still needs to be learned about the indications for use, the correct dosage, the side effects as well as the short- and long-range results.

Massive daily doses of vitamin B_3 (niacin or Niacinamide) for one year for autistic, schizophrenic and epileptic children, research shows, produced no significant results (Roukema and Emery 1970).

A research psychologist reported marked improvement from prescriptions of five vitamins in massive doses in 200 schizophrenic and autistic children during a treatment period of four months (Rimland 1970).

Another psychiatrist, using several vitamins, reported good results over a five-year period in calming hyperactive learning-disabled children. He states that a controlled study is presently underway, with results due in 1972 (Cott 1970, Cott 1971).

Another psychiatrist reported improvement in schizophrenics by the use of megavitamin therapy—also known as the ortho-molecular method. He stressed that the megavitamins are in addition to other therapeutic measures and did not replace them (Hawkins 1971).

Additional references to the use of vitamin therapy in schizophrenia are given in the book, *Mental Health through Nutrition* (Blaine 1969).

Conclusion on Megavitamins

Present evidence concerning the usefulness of megavitamin therapy further points out the need for additional controlled clinical research. Like anything new in the field of science, this procedure will have to be adequately tested and proven for a period of time before it will be generally accepted.

The stimulating excitement of pioneering in any field has a positive effect on people who are seeking answers to the unknown, or who are searching for complete solutions to complicated problems. However, the same pioneering tends to produce a negative effect on the skeptic, the doubter and the insecure encumbered with inertia and the status quo. Constructive criticism from people who have an open but guarded mind should always be heard and gratefully received. But narrow, critical remarks filled with pride and prejudice are pitiable when they are issued by men and women who are supposed to be professional, scientific and charitable in helping their patients solve problems.

Organic, inorganic—any difference?

The subjects of nutrition and megavitamin prescriptions are controversial enough but the debate between the Organic and Inorganic is explosive with feelings running high.

Consumer trends today are fast shifting to the "natural" or "organic" products in everything from fertilizers to cosmetics. Do scientific facts support the need? Or is it a fad being fanned by the winds of emotion rising around the ecological issues?

It is most urgent, of course, that we clean up our environment and eliminate as much as possible all inorganic and organic poisons and pollutants. But at the same time, it is also of the utmost importance that we discern properly. After all, the body needs certain inorganic chemicals for proper nutrition. It is not necessary to junk all cars because some cause death or are not fit for the road.

Take, for example, the soil. It is a mixture of both organic and inorganic matter. However, agriculturalists tell us that the roots of trees, plants, grasses, herbs, weeds, etc., *do not absorb a single organic compound.* Micro-organisms in the soil population break down the organic matter, whether it occurs naturally or is placed there as organic fertilizer by the farmer, into inorganic matter of chemicals and *the roots absorb and take in only inorganic chemicals* such as nitrogen, phosphorus, potassium, calcium, magnesium, sulphur and others. The plant then builds its own organic compounds with the chemicals from the soil plus the chemicals, like carbon dioxide, which the leaves take out of the air (Martin and Ervin).

There are advantages and disadvantages to both organic and inorganic fertilizers. Each is needed to obtain proper soil for plant growth. Organic fertilizers are low in nitrogen, thus the yield of the plant is reduced and the nutrient content is not improved. If inorganic fertilizers are applied in too large amounts then salt injury may result to the plant.

Hydroponics—growing plants in water to which inorganic chemical substances have been added—is as nutritious as food grown in good soil (Hoagland and Arnon 1965).

The same insect pests attack plants, regardless of what type of fertilizer was used (Gowans and Rauschkolb 1971).

There is no scientific proof that organically grown foods are better than those grown conventionally (Schweigert 1971, Saltman 1971). If there is proper scientific proof that the organically grown food is better then this author would be very happy to see it and so would the professors who are being quoted in the article of reference.

If the organicists refers to decreased food value resulting from processing techniques that remove valuable nutrients, then there is no argument. What is true of foods is also true of vitamins. Professor Linus Pauling says that pure ascorbic acid (Ascorbic Acid U.S.P., L-Ascorbic Acid, Vitamin C) whether it be synthetically produced or that which is present in natural foods is identical (Pauling 1970).

"Synthetic vitamins are identical in all respects to those occurring in foods," as stated on page 171, Vol. 23, of Colliers Encyclopedia.

The customer pays a good deal more for organic foodstuffs and for organic vitamins. Each person involved must decide for himself. Most of us make emotional decisions and overlook or disregard the facts. Check your emotions on a financial scale and see if you are really getting your money's worth.

Also, check the scientific data on both sides of this potentially hot issue. This author is interested in true scientific facts and would welcome research evidence supporting the organic claims. If it is really better and fits one's financial budget, then it would be the logical route to take.

Conclusion

Nutrition is important and more is being learned all the time. This material must be learned and applied to the role of assistance in learning, behavior and disease. One cannot overemphasize the need of a balanced diet which includes proper and controlled snacking.

The director of the U.S. Department of Agriculture (USDA) warns that gaps in knowledge about human nutritional requirements aren't being filled rapidly enough. As a result, many food fads are proposed, gain acceptance and will likely continue until nutritionists are able to add substantially to the existing data (Gortner 1972).

When they are needed, dietary nutrient supplements (protein, vitamins, minerals, etc) should be used in a positive way. Allergic foods should be removed in the same way to insure the best possible function of the human body.

Medication still plays a vital role in the lives of children with learning-behavior disabilities, even when good nutrition is present with or without dietary additions of protein supplements, vitamins and minerals.

If diet alone could accomplish the desired effects our work would be easy indeed.

BIBLIOGRAPHY FOR CHAPTER SEVENTEEN

Blaine, T. R., *Mental Health through Nutrition,* chapters 4-6, pp. 49-95, The Citadel Press, New York, 1969.

Citizens Board of Inquiry into Hunger and Malnutrition in the United States, *Hunger U.S.A.,* chapter 2, p. 31, Beacon Press, Boston, 1968.

Clemis, Jack D., Dizziness and Deafness Traced to Diet, *Medical World News,* pp. 34E-34F, Oct. 22, 1971.

Cott, Allan, Abstract: Vitamin Treatment: Positive Results, *Behavior Today Newsletter,* Vol. 1, no. 28, p. 2, Dec. 21, 1970.

Cott, Allan, A Hyperactive Child Needs Nutrients, Not Drugs, *Prevention,* pp. 169-176, April, 1971.

Council on Foods and Nutrition, Zen Macrobiotic Diets, *Journal of the American Medical Association,* Vol. 218, No. 3, p. 397, Oct. 18, 1971.

Goldstein, M. L., High-Dose Ascorbic Acid Therapy, *Journal of the American Medical Association,* Vol. 216, No. 2, p. 332, April 12, 1971.

Gortner, Willis A., Leanness of Data Hinders Nutrition Research, *Journal of the American Medical Association,* Medical News, Vol. 219, No. 1, p. 16, Jan. 3, 1972.

Gowans, K.D., and **Rauschkolb,** R. S., Organic and Inorganic Fertilizers and Soil Amendments, Agricultural Extension, University of California, Brochure AXT-357, August, 1971.

Hawkins, David R., Back to Reality the Megavitamin Way, *Medical World News,* pp. 15-18, Sept. 24, 1971.

Hoagland, D. R., and **Arnon,** D. I., The Water Culture Method for Growing Plants without Soil, Circular 347, The College of Agriculture, University of California, Berkeley, 1965.

Martin, James P., and **Ervin,** Jarel O., Soil Organisms—Fact or Fiction, Division of Soils and Plant Nutrition, University of California Citrus Experiment Station, Riverside, California.

Pauling, Linus, *Vitamin C and the Common Cold,* chapter 7, pp. 69-70, W. H. Freeman & Co., San Francisco, 1970.
Ibid., chapter 4, p. 30.

Rimland, Bernard, Abstract: Vitamin Treatment: Positive Results, *Behavior Today Newsletter,* Vol. 1, No. 28, p. 2, Dec. 21, 1970.

Roukema, Richard, and **Emery,** Louise, Abstract: Vitamin Therapy: Negative Results, *Behavior Today: Findings,* Research Supplement, Vol. 1, No. 28, p. B, Dec. 21, 1970.

Saltman, Paul D., Professor of Biology, University of California, San Diego, Weird Diets Worry Nutrition Expert, Part VI, p. 3, *Los Angeles Times,* April 1, 1971.

Schweigert, Bernard S., Chairman, Department of Food Science and Technology, University of California at Davis, Poison or packed with Nutrients, *Los Angeles Times,* March 18, 1971.

Speer, Frederic, *Allergy of the Nervous System,* Charles C. Thomas Publisher, 1970.
Ibid., chapter 7, pp. 122-133.
Ibid., chapter 10, pp. 198-199.
Ibid., Table XIII, p. 203.

Sleisenger, M. H., **Weser,** E., **Bayless,** Theodore M., **Rosensweig,** Norton S., **Huang,** Shi-Shung, **Simoons,** Frederick, and **McCracken,** Robert D., Milk Drinking and Lactase Deficiency, *Roche Image of Medicine and Research,* pp. 6-9, International Medical Press, Inc., New York, Oct., 1971.

Udenfriend, Sidney, director, Roche Institute of Molecular Biology, To Learn More About Life Processes, *Medical World News,* p. 49, Oct. 15, 1971.

Ungar, George, New Concepts of the Biochemistry of the Mind, *Roche Image of Medicine and Research,* Vol. 13, No. 6, pp. 3-4, Sept., 1971.

Weirs, J. M., and **Kaufman,** H. S., A Subtle Organic Component in Some Cases of Mental Illness, *Archives of General Psychiatry,* Vol. 25, pp. 74-78, July 1971.

Wenck, Dorothy A., Snacking: Fun or Folly, *Today's Homemaker Newsletter,* Orange County Home Advisor, University of California, Agricultural Extension Service, April, 1970.

Wenck, Dorothy A., Our Changing Food Habits, Orange County Home Advisor, *Today's Homemaker Newsletter,* University of California, Agricultural Extension Service, April 10, 1968.

CHAPTER EIGHTEEN

RANDOM THOUGHTS FROM A DOCTOR'S DIARY

As each of us accumulates observations we store the information in mental bins, so to speak. Some bins become more prominent than others. A pile-up of data in one bin causes the observer to think, ponder and formulate ideas or hazy opinions about the meaning of the mass of details.

Following this, a certain amount of frustration occurs when specific questions present themselves: Has someone else made the same observations and arrived at similar opinions? Has any formal research been carried out on the subject? Where can help be found to check the volumes of reports, papers, theses, abstractions, etc., that are appearing in greater and greater abundance?

This chapter shares with the reader various observations and opinions made by the author for which there may be little or no specific scientific substantiation.

Ear Muffs in Sunny California

Two children with a high degree of auditory distractibility are profiting today from special ear muffs to protect their hearing from excessive noise. The ear gear is not designed to salvage the hearing of the child but to filter out the noise so he can concentrate on his school work in a special class. What is routine noise for other students becomes quite excessive for this child whose auditory system apparently amplifies sound far beyond normal proportions. The resulting distraction makes school work impossible for the child. He wears them, however, only when engaged in school assignments. One child, after a couple of months, is being slowly weaned from the ear muffs as he gradually develops a more normal response to auditory stimuli.

Mirror Writing, Reversals and Ritalin®

Visual perception problems can be treated with appropriate visual perceptual techniques. However, to the normal prescription can be observed a few exceptions. These only prove the rule.

In a few children for whom methylphenidate HCL (Ritalin®) was prescribed to reduce overactivity, this medication produced the added benefit of correcting the problem of reversing the letters b and d in the case of one boy 14 years old. A boy and a girl had their reversals ("mirror writing") corrected in just a few weeks.

The benefits of Ritalin® for another boy were remarkably demonstrated when the lad ran out of his supply. During the few days when he was off the drug he began to reverse his letters, only to have the reversing disappear when Ritalin® was restored.

A third case involves a seven-year-old boy named Burt. He did not have any reversing problem until he was placed on Ritalin®. The problem ceased when the medication was discontinued.

The elusive reaction caused by Ritalin® is quite intriguing. The drug should not be considered a cure-all in the treatment of visual perceptual problems.

The Paradoxical Reactions of Stimulants

The average person is stimulated by a stimulant. But 60 to 80 per cent of overactive children and adults are calmed by stimulants. Some take it in the morning and at night and are calmed both times. Others can take it only during the day for its calming effect because the medicine taken in late afternoon or evening stimulates them.

What mysterious biochemical changes occur in these patients as the day wears on that causes such a dramatic shift?

A third type, whose nervous system is so sluggish, have a nearly uncontrollable tendency to go to sleep throughout the day, even when they are well rested. This condition is called "Narcolepsy." Dexedrine® and Ritalin® are the medicines which can help in this case. They keep the patient awake and alert without giving him any stimulating sensation.

Thus in one neurological problem stimulants calm the overactive; in another neurological problem they arouse the underactive. What a paradox!

TV's Role in Learning Disabilities

The senses of seeing, hearing and touching all working together help the mind to learn. Remove the sense of touch and learning is greatly reduced.

This is precisely what happens as a child watches a telecast. He looks and hears, but he does not touch. What's more, he sits, keeping his skeletal system inactive (unless he wiggles and fidgets a lot).

The "boob-tube" is a poor excuse for a baby sitter, even though it is convenient and economical. TV is here to stay, of course, so the problem cannot be corrected by eliminating the electronic gadget from our culture. But a wise parent can take two courses of action. One is to put strict limits on viewing time, causing youngsters to spend more time in activities that involve touch and body motion as well as sight and sound. The other is to have TV programs designed for viewer participation. These programs would then involve the child in the very game, lesson, plaything, etc., that is featured on the program. If notified ahead of time, parents can purchase the economical materials to be used during the program.

In addition, there is no substitute for personal, active involvement in most learning situations. It's important to "keep in touch." And tele(sound) vision(sight) could add a significant "touch."

Internal and External Shock and Memory

Dr. David Krech (1968), professor of psychology at the University of California at Berkeley, describes in his article, "The Chemistry of Learning," what is called the two-stage memory storage process theory.

Stage one, according to the psychologist, is a short-term electrochemical memory process established in the brain after every experience. After a brief period the short-term process triggers the second or long-term protein-enzymatic process for the memory. This primarily involves the production of new proteins and the induction of higher enzymatic activity levels in the brain cells.

The article goes on to relate how Dr. Murray Jarvick would erase the short-term electrochemical memory of rats by passing a mild electric current across the brain of the animal. On the other hand, the mild electrical shock would have no erasing effect on the long-term protein-enzymatic memory. Thus a mild electrical shock from an external source can erase the short memory.

Medical specialists are aware that the Electro-shock Therapy (EST) which passes a relatively strong electrical current through the frontal or psychic area of the brain helps to erase overloaded negative memories in certain types of mental illness.

The author is of the opinion that in the same way that these external electrical sources stop and interfere with the memory, internal abnormal electrical discharges in the human brain, as evidenced on abnormal EEG (brain wave test) tracings in the form of spikes, sharp waves, paroxysmal bursts and the like, also can interfere with the memory process.

Those who have convulsive seizures (epilepsy) also sustain varying degrees of memory loss for events immediately preceding the episode. In these cases the internal abnormal electrical discharge is great enough to produce the convulsive reaction of the patient's muscles as in the grand mal type.

There is another type of seizure patient who, although without a clinical seizure or convulsion, has an EEG which shows definite sub-clinical seizure activity. This prevents the proper functioning of the area of the brain where the abnormal pattern is located, if allowed to go on unchecked (Hutt, Lee and Ounsted 1963). It also has an adverse effect on adjacent normal areas, according to Eugene B. Spitz, M.D., former associate professor in charge of pediatric neurosurgery at the University of Pennsylvania Medical School, Philadelphia, Pennsylvania. Griffith and Davidson (1970) observed improved IQ's in 5 out of 12 patients who had undergone hemispherectomies for intractable seizures.

This discussion does not center in the slightest degree on clinical convulsive problems, although there are certain analogous features. Nor is neuro-surgery being advocated for those with learning disabilities. Instead, this section deals with a person who hears or sees something to be remembered but in whom a few seconds afterward an internal, abnormal electrical discharge in the hearing or seeing center of the brain quickly erases the short-term memory of the input.

Another possible interruption of memory can occur on the same basis: an internal abnormal electrical discharge could erase the area of the brain which handles organized recall, located on the lateral and basal part of the left temporal lobe. The discharge erases the information just as it rises to the conscious level of thought and just before the person can use it in speech or writing. After a while, the same information can again be recalled because it was not erased from the long-term memory process—just from the specific recall area.

Neurology and Delinquency

Behind drug addiction, crime, juvenile delinquency, alcoholism, psychosis and welfarism lies a large area directly involved with the study of neurology. These problems are quite complex. Neurology should not be overlooked in the diagnoses and therapeutic programs suggested for these types of people.

Certain characteristics of people caught up in these problems appear common to them all, as this simplified list shows:

1   Home problems, such as divorce, quarreling, unhappy parents, poor emotional climate, parental rejection, parental overindulgence, etc.

2   School failure in spite of a normal IQ for many. (The author worked for six years with drug addicts. Their disparaging descriptions of school learning and their behavior problems are consistently recited. A high percentage of school learning problems are neurological.

3   Low or poor self-concept resulting in an inferiority complex for which they compensate through drug excess, delinquent and criminal

behavior, or passively through alcoholism, welfarism and withdrawal into the psychotic world. This low concept of self can come from the home situation, the school situation or from both.

4   The percentage of abnormal EEGs is high among felons, murderers, psychotics and fairly high among delinquents. Errant EEGs are also found commonly among students with a learning disability.

A feature that applies only to certain cases of schizophrenic types of psychosis is the multi-sensory neurological perceptual problem that hinders a person from proper contact with physical reality. It can result also in other neurological types of problems, such as severe hyperkinesis that causes poor learning even in a student with a bright, superior or genius IQ.

The similarity of these various features to neurological learning problems raises the logical question: What percentage of these differing problems could be helped by *adding* the proper neurological approach? A rough estimate (pertaining to addicts where the greatest amount of contact has been made) would be approximately 20 per cent.

Protein-enzyme synthesis is part of the memory system. One part of an enzyme is protein, the other part is often directly derived from a vitamin. Antigens and antibodies, which have to do with the body's resistance to allergic and infectious invaders, are protein.

Chronic illnesses were found in 15 per cent of the mothers whose children had learning disabilities, but in the control group the percentage was zero (Meier 1971). Protein-deficient diets in rats resulted in offspring who had small brains, learning disorders and severe emotional problems (Zamenhof, van Martheus and Grauel 1971). In the author's thinking, this suggests an urgent need for more precise knowledge concerning the specific protein requirements in pregnancy for the mother and her unborn child, especially in the early life of the infant. We should persist in our research to determine precisely what essential—and even what non-essential—amino acids are required for the learning process during these very critical stages of brain development. What quantities are needed for the various types of metabolism and functions of different people? For example, the hyperactive might well need more than the average normal, active child, and so on. These questions present a challenge, to say the least, for some enterprising bio-neuro-physio-chemist team.

Does the Neurological Approach Also Help Adults?

All the remedies suggested for children apply also to adults. There is an adult hyperkinetic syndrome because only a few hyperkinetic children automatically grow out of their overactivity problem. Many who do not overcome their problems are able to cover up with an adult facade.

The percentage of good results among adult patients ranges from 40 to 50 per cent. In children the percentage of recovery is much higher. Since many adults manage to mask the various aspects of their problem their symptoms can appear to be quite different from as well as quite similar to those of children. Associated emotional problems, rather than neurological ones, may be the main symptoms presented. Any problem that continues unchecked and without proper care is almost certain to become more involved and increase in severity. Thus the longer the duration of the illness the longer and perhaps also the more complex the treatment program.

Robert A. Ingram, M.D., of Orange, Texas, refers to older people with neurological problems as "minimal brain dysfunctional adults." A letter from Dr. Ingram was printed in the November 1970 *Medical World News*. In this missive the physician correlates the Minnesota Multiphasic Personality Inventory (MMPI) with the EEG (brain wave test).

Frank R. Ervin, M.D., who heads the psychiatric research laboratory at the Massachusetts General Hospital in Boston, correlates violent attacks by people with their erratic pattern of electrical activity in the brain. Dr. Ervin states that the childhood history of violent people reveals hyperactivity, multiple fire-setting, prolonged enuresis (bed wetting), cruelty to animals and destructive activities generally greater than their peers (Rosenthal, 1970).

Thirty out of 50 case histories among the author's active adult patients offer the following information.

Females: 13   Males: 17

Ages: 18-63 (12 in their thirties, 10 in their forties).

Following are the eight most common symptoms with their frequency. In checking an appropriate symptom, the patient stated that they had it "continually," or "on and off," and they also checked whether it was for "all of their lives," or "most of their lives."

26 were nervous

21 were depressed

20 were irritable

19 were tense inside

18 were anxious

17 had headache problems

16 had sleep problems

15 had temper problems

A total of 12 symptoms was charted. The average symptom per person was 6.4.

Electroencephalographic (EEG) findings noted:

3 were normal

2 were borderline abnormalities

24 were minimally abnormal

1 was severely abnormal

20 out of the 30 had temporal area involvement. "Spiking" was the abnormality in 15 out of the 20 with temporal area involvement.

7 had diffuse abnormality

5 had a diffuse plus other abnormalities

Only 1 had a latent petit mal pattern.

Medication offered mostly good results with some fair results and, in the case of one patient, no results at all.

22 were on Dilantin®

7 were on Stelazine®

5 were on Valium®

6 were on Ritalin®

4 were on Dexedrine®

1 was on d-amphetamine SO_4

4 were on Obotan®

2 were on Desoxyn®

1 was on Aventyl®

It is interesting to note that these stimulant medications produced the paradoxical calming effect in these adults.

The adult hyperkinetic syndrome is a clinical entity with rewarding therapeutic results for at least half of them. It will be an eyebrow-raising surprise to many that such symptoms as depression, anxiety, nervousness, irritability, tenseness and temper can be not only psychogenic but also neurogenic in origin.

An Appeal for Empathy

A person with good visual-motor control of their fingers loses that control when he views his writing hand by means of a delayed image response TV screen circuit, rather than by the customary direct eye viewing. By this technique, a person with normal abilities can actually experience the frustrations of one who cannot control his fingers well enough to write.

The delayed TV apparatus is pictured and described in the book, *Eye and Brain* (Gregory 1966). No one who has ever used the machine will criticize a person with visual perceptual problems.

The opinions and observations of this chapter have been shared in good faith to stimulate thought and research on behalf of the handicapped.

Constructive comments and data would be most welcomed, whether they bolster or challenge the ideas and theories herein presented. Those few readers, and there are always a few, who would write for spite or rancor about the content of this chapter might save themselves and others the time and negative effort involved.

Remember: the knock of hostile criticism abroad in the world usually indicates that no previous "knock" through adequate inquiry has been made. BUT the exchange of meaningful material between the searchers of purposeful truth helps build better tools of therapy that serve needy adults and youth.

BIBLIOGRAPHY FOR CHAPTER EIGHTEEN

Gregory, R. L., *Eye and Brain, the Psychology of Seeing,* World University Library, pp. 216-217, McGraw-Hill Book Co., New York, 1966.

Griffith, H., and **Davidson,** M., Review: Brain Functions, by **Rosner,** Burton S., *Annual Review of Psychology,* Vol. 21, p. 573, Edited by Farnsworth, P. R., *Annual Reviews,* Palo Alto, 1970. Original Article: Long-Term Changes in Intellect and Behavior After Hemispherectomy, *Journal of Neurosurgery and Psychiatry,* Vol. 29, pp. 571-576, 1966.

Hutt, S. J., **Lee,** D., and **Ounsted,** C., Review: Disorders of Storage and Retrieval, Central Processing Dysfunctions in Children: A Review of Research, p. 66; **Chalfant,** James C., and **Scheffelin,** Margaret A., *NINDS* Monograph Series, U.S. Department of Health, Education and Welfare, 1969. Original Article: Digit Memory and Evoked Discharges in Four Light-Sensitive Epileptic Children, *Developmental Medicine and Child Neurology,* Vol. 5, pp. 561-571, 1963.

Krech, David, The Chemistry of Learning, *Saturday Review,* pp. 48-50, January 20, 1968.

Meier, John H., Prevalence and Characteristics of Learning Disabilities Found in Second Grade Children, *Journal of Learning Disabilities,* Vol. 4, No. 1, p. 11, Jan., 1971.

Rosenthal, Alan, Violence Is Predictable, *Today's Health,* pp. 56-57, 71-73, Nov., 1970.

Zamenhof, Stephen, **van Martheus,** Edith, and **Grauel,** Ludmila, Abstract: Inherited Effects of Poor Diet, *Behavior Today,* p. 2, June 28, 1971, Original Article: DNA (Cell Number) in Neonatal Brain: Second Generation (F_2) Alteration by Maternal (F_0) Dietary Protein Restriction, *Science,* Vol. 172, pp. 850-851, May 21, 1971.

CHAPTER NINETEEN

THE SPIRITUAL IMPLICATIONS
OF LEARNING DISABILITIES

To augment our consideration of the "whole person" concept presented in chapter two, this final section is included. No one is obligated to read it. Belief in a Supreme Being should not be forced upon anyone. However, a sincere sharing of one's personal faith and how it relates to our subject provides an opportunity for the seeker to examine the issue for himself.

Man is incurably religious. No tribe, society or nation is without its form of worship.

In recent years, religion courses in America at the college and university levels have become some of the most popular (Time 1971).

Arnold Toynbee, acknowledged to be the world's greatest living historian, believes that religion involves "the emotional and moral facets of the human psyche above all, but the intellectual facet as well."

Writing in the preface to John Cogley's (1968) *Search for Final Meaning,* Toynbee declares that religion "extends to the whole of Man's World; it is not limited to that part of it which is accessible to the human senses and which can therefore be studied scientifically and can be manipulated by technology."

A human being's religious concern, in Toynbee's view, "leads him to ask questions that cannot be answered in terms of common sense or of science. . . . He has to find answers to these baffling questions in order to take the action that he has to take in consequence in his being alive. These answers . . . give him a chart or picture of the world in which he finds himself, including the part of it—perhaps the most important part—that is beyond the ken of both common sense and science."

And so man continues to reach out toward his Creator. Those who are wise enough to cultivate a meaningful relationship between sacred and secular life are rewarded many times over. In practical ways, for example, it can be noted that people who seldom go to church have twice the incidence of fatal heart disease than do faithful churchgoers (Slovut

1970); children who are faithful in Sunday school rarely become criminals. A business man who learns to pray and commit his business to God will reap extra dividends.

Faith is not blind acceptance. Rather, it is open-eyed trust in something that has a measurable value of potential. Faith and trust are reinforced when the promised results can be experienced. Belief is further enhanced when the directions of faith and trust are received on a personal basis.

In most religions, such directions are written. Therefore, those who cannot read or who are poor readers will not be able to have as direct a contact as those who can read well. Good listening takes a person only so far. Imagine two husbands away from home on a trip. Which one will enjoy most a love letter from his wife, the good listener or the good reader?

The Christian Church has gradually become a good listener instead of a good proclaimer of its message, a religious sociologist told a gathering of churchmen in Denver. Peter L. Berger, quoted in the October 11, 1971 issue of *Time* magazine, said, "If there is any stance that has marked the Christian community in recent years, it is that of listening." I wonder, how many are only listening because they are poor readers?

Listening in order to understand others is fine, Berger declared, "but too many Christians are listening to an entity known as 'modern man' in the expectation that thence will come the redemptive word." This kind of listening, he concluded, is demoralizing.

In summary, Berger told his fellow churchmen: "Ages of faith are not marked by dialogue, but by proclamation."

In our chapter on counseling, the matter was brought out concerning an adequate self-concept based upon certain psychological factors related to self and to those in authority. The discussion was placed on a relatively inadequate basis because its success depended upon fallible people such as parents, peers and one's own self.

But there is an absolute adequate self-concept based upon God and His Word (Wagner). The essential pillars of this absolute self-concept are provided in spiritual conversion as a part of the blessing of salvation. They are separate from one's own personal efforts or merits. True spiritual conversion is basically one's rejection or surrender of self-sovereignty and the acceptance of God's sovereignty.

Resources of Faith

1 An essential belonging or sense of acceptance, the "I'm in!" feeling, is provided in the love of God the Father. John 16:27 states, "The Father himself loves you. . . ."

Spiritual belongingness comes from a sense of being related to the One who owns us (I Cor. 6:19, 20). We are His; we belong to Him (John 10:27). We are all His children and members of His body, the Church universal (Eph. 5:30). This belongingness is provided by His grace and is not based upon our being good enough to merit it.

Out of this relationship comes the love response that motivates true obedience from the heart (John 14:15; 15:14; I John 4:8-12). After spiritual conversion we can love others for themselves and have a sense of belonging with them because we accept the sovereign rule of God the Father over all mankind, especially over those of the "household of faith." He is not only our Father, but He is the God of everyone else. The things that others do that frustrate us are first known and permitted by God. For this reason we assume no essential authority over others or over our circumstances to correct people or to resent what is happening. By the love of God the Father is provided essential belonging with Him and people.

2   The essential worthiness or sense of worth, the "I'm good, clean, right" feeling is provided in the grace of God the Son. Romans 8:1 declares, "There is therefore now no condemnation for those who are in Christ Jesus."

Guilt is a feeling of being wrong. In God's plan, the person who has transgressed can come to God and admit his transgression and find forgiveness and cleansing of conscience (I John 1:9). When a person holds himself responsible to God for his conduct more than to his own ideals or to social opinion, he can find a realistic release from the guilt suffered by the transgression. But when a person exalts the importance of his own ideals or of social opinion above the authority of God's Word, he then takes upon himself the authority to exercise disciplinary punishment upon himself for his transgression. This self-condemnation and self-rejection is confused with wholesome self-discipline and the person blocks the release from guilt that comes through confession of sin to God and the statement of His forgiveness (I John 1:9). It is illogical for one to be able to punish himself enough for his own errors so that he could feel sufficiently clean from guilt to respect himself when in the self-punishing process he is constantly rejecting himself with feelings of total disgust for his normal reactions to life situations.

The Christian who finds himself in this irrational whirlpool of thought needs to return to the simple but profound provision of the Bible. God in Christ has not only forgiven his past sins but provided for the forgiveness of all sins (I John 2:2). God has justified the Christian so that he never again will be subject to condemnation for sin (Romans 8:1, 31-34). The Christian who is condemning himself is dishonoring what God has established as forgiven and clean. He is presuming a role of judgment upon himself that is beyond the will of God. "What God has cleansed, no longer consider unholy" (Acts 10:15). Hence in God's forgiveness, based upon the gracious redemptive work of Christ the Son, man has available to him a realistic basis for his essential sense of worthiness (Ephesians 1:6).

3   The essential competence or sense of self-competence, the "I can" feeling is provided in the communion of God the Holy Spirit. II Corinthians 13:14 tells the believer, "The grace of the Lord Jesus Christ, and the love of God, and the fellowship of the Holy Spirit, be with you all." Ephesians 3:16 promises, "that He (the Father) would grant you, according to the riches of His glory, to be strengthened with power through His Spirit in the inner man." God promises to oversee the life situations of His children and exert a controlling influence. God is always working circumstances together for good (Romans 8:28). He is a good God (James 1:17). He is faithful (I Corinthians 10:13) in all situations to adjust the ratio between the stress of the situation and the person's strength to resist so that His children can by faith in Him always be victorious. The difficulties of life to the Christian all have a wholesome purpose, to exercise faith in God, and this exercise is necessary for spiritual growth (Heb. 5:14; 12:11; James 1:2-4; I Peter 1:6-9). The Christian need not fear any situation for God the Holy Spirit is always with him (John 14:16-18; Isaiah 41:10) to provide whatever he needs to face that situation, and the situation already has been regulated so it will not destroy the Christian completely. The situation belongs to God, and the Christian also belongs to God, and God promises to abide with His child all the way through the situation to provide whatever is needed. God is glorified in the life of the Christian in this way. He will never lead a Christian into any situation He will not also lead him through, and He assures that the end result will be good, whether the experience was a pleasant one or not. Thus the Christian has a resource for an inner sense of essential competence in facing any future situation of life (Philippians 4:13). The Christian who is fearful is one who is not thus sensing God's presence in the varying situations of life. He feels too responsible for his own welfare. But the Christian is never dealing with forces beyond the control of the One who is controlling him!

Even if it were possible for a person to build a totally adequate self-concept based upon his own physical, psychological, emotional, intellectual and social attitudes, the concept would still be relative. Being relative, it would be inadequate because everyone finally perishes and leaves all behind.

Realistically, the relative self-concept of most of us is poor at best. But whether good or poor, each one needs and can have the absolute eternally adequate self-concept which is guaranteed imperishable by the Almighty Creator Himself.

As a medical doctor working in a scientific world, the author desires to share the relevance of his personal faith. That faith and trust rests in the God of the Bible, declared to be the Word of God, and in His Son the Lord Jesus Christ, who is God manifested in human flesh. This faith in Jesus Christ as personal Lord and Saviour resulted from learning about His great love for me, though I was totally undeserving. This faith has proven itself personally, in married and family life, socially and in the medical profession.

The same results often accompany a sharing of this faith. I have shared it with people in Africa, Europe, throughout North America, with the poor, middle class, and with wealthy persons. I have shared it with the moral person as well as the criminal, the alcoholic, and the addict. The message, when believed, always produces the same deliverance from guilt, the tremendous ego boost of being loved, accepted and cared for by Almighty God on a personal basis, the knowledge of sins forgiven, the source of daily help, strength and guidance for the physical, emotional intellectual, social and spiritual joys and problems of life. In addition to that and more there is the sure hope of the return of the Lord Jesus to take those who have trusted Him to be forever with Him ruling and reigning in His vast eternal universe.

Any who will receive Christ, the Messiah, the Anointed of God as personal Saviour from sins, becomes a member of His family through the regenerating work and power of the Holy Spirit of God. If you would desire further clarification on how to believe in and receive the Lord Jesus Christ personally then please write and a booklet will be mailed to you.

But to return to the religious implication regarding your child's learning problem:

The experience could be God-ordained to teach you something worthwhile. We humans often forget God when everything is going along according to our designs. But problems beyond our ability to control can cause us to look up. Patience is learned in trying situations; understanding and wisdom are best developed when we call upon God for guidance in problems which we cannot handle. God delights to strengthen our faith in Him with His answers to our requests for help.

When parents must seek the resources of God on behalf of a child with a severe learning disability their lives often become a living testimony to others. Afterward they can empathize with others in similar circumstances and become a source of help to them.

Just as a learning disability can interfere with physical and mental growth, spiritual disinterest and neglect can rob a person of wisdom, knowledge and understanding of God Who is the very source of all human resources.

"The fear of the Lord is the beginning of knowledge," we are reminded in Proverbs 1:7. "The fear of the Lord is the beginning of wisdom, and the knowledge of the Holy One is understanding" (Proverbs 9:10). "But if any of you lack wisdom, let him ask of God, who gives to all men generously and without reproach, and it will be given to him" (James 1:5).

The basic rules guiding man's relationship with man are virtually the same among all great religions of the world. They teach that man is to worship and obey God. But in most cases man is expected to accomplish this on his own, yet man throughout history has failed his fellow man and God over and over again. Only true Biblical Christianity offers freely a source outside ourselves which a person can receive to help him relate properly both to God and to man. The same pride that keeps a parent from admitting his child has a learning problem might also lock him into a "do-it-yourself" religious tradition which is totally powerless to achieve the life of joy and victory which God has promised to all who love and trust Him. The proud person attempts to earn favor with God through good works, rather than to admit that he is imperfect, sinful and in need of help.

History's greatest periods resulted from mutual benefit following a true spiritual awakening in which the whole person reaped physical, psychological and spiritual blessings.

The awful blotches on the pages of history marked by wars in the name of religion were, in reality, the acts of proud men fighting for tradition, rather than the acts of truly just and peaceable men who found their peace with God through Jesus Christ.

Jesus Christ said of the religious people in His day that they had perceptual problems of a visual and auditory nature. He said that they had ears to hear but couldn't hear . . . eyes to see but could not see (Matthew 13:14,15). Whether their perceptual problems were neurological or psychological it is not possible now to discern. Nevertheless, they could not perceive their problems and thus were incapable of helping themselves or others.

Occasionally parents with certain religious convictions refuse specialized help for their child with a learning problem. The reason they give is that they feel they should trust God alone to care for the matter.

Could it be that these people are forgetting a basic principle concerning God's method of working? God delights to work through people. The God-given means they possess is basically spiritual, psychological or physical. God speaks to us through His Word, for example, that has been printed by men. Most believers heard from some other person that God loved them and had a plan of salvation for them. Certain kinds of people will take penicillin for a sore throat but will refuse counsel and medicine for an emotional or a learning problem.

Evaluate your position. If you have resisted the efforts of others to help, see if it is not time now to change so that your youngster may receive help before it is too late.

Our world is filled with amazing scientific discoveries and accomplishment resulting from the exploits of the human mind. Such achievements cause man to be proud, to take credit for the feats and to inflate his philosophy of humanism. For such individuals it should be pointed out that their function as a complex human being would be useless without the soul and the spirit to energize and direct their efforts.

But suppose a skeptic searched diligently and found an invention man had made which apparently had no prototype in nature.

"Ah!" he would say, "here is that exception that destroys the argument of God's prior claim on everything. This is strictly a product of the human brain."

Look at that brain once again for a moment: It is a most impressive organ. Scattered over our bodies are some 200,000 living thermometer cells, a half million pressure-sensing cells and three or four million pain-sensing cells. The electrical signals from all of these, plus the signals from the eyes, ears, nose and areas sensitive to taste and touch are all routed to the brain where the welter of impulses is sorted, stored, and acted upon. The human brain contains a hundred times as many nerve lines as all the telephone systems of the world put together. It is the information center of our bodies, an exalted sort of electrical computer, an assemblage of switchboard that correlates sensory signals and determines what action the body should take.

Yes, the human brain is a wonderful device. But man did not plan it or develop it. He only uses it to plan and develop other things. This means that since God planned and developed the human brain, all the good that this organ produces is indirectly the result of the Master Who created its complex facility. Evil emanates from it because of man's rebellion against, or failure to conform to, God's ways.

Since man owes his powers, indeed his very existence, to God, can he say that he has a claim upon his own life superior to God's claim? Of course not! God has prior claim.

The divine truth leads us to recognize the possibility of infringement upon that claim. Our very failure to recognize God's claim is an infringement upon it. There are penalties for such violations, just as there are penalties for infringing on a patent or copyright in our society.

However, God prefers not to penalize or to press charges. "Let the wicked forsake his way, and the unrighteous man his thoughts: and let him return to the Lord, and He will have compassion on him; and to our God, for He will abundantly pardon." (Isaiah 55:7)

Indeed, God goes even further: "But God demonstrates His own love toward us, in that while we were yet sinners, Christ died for us." (Romans 5:8)

Is it intelligent to neglect this claim which sprang from the love of the Creator?

BIBLIOGRAPHY FOR CHAPTER NINETEEN

Cogley, John, *Search for Final Meaning,* Preface by **Toynbee,** Arnold, Vol. III, pp. 441-456, Britannica Perspective, Encyclopoedia Britannica, Inc., Chicago, 1968.

Slovut, Gordon, Faith May Be Healthy, *The Minneapolis Star,* Dec. 14, 1970.

Time magazine, The Boom in Religion Studies, pp. 83-84, Oct. 18, 1971.

Wagner, Maurice, *The Building of an Adequate Self-Concept,* Manuscript being readied for publication, Los Angeles, Calif.

Holy Bible (NAS) Acts, chapter 10, verse 15, The Lockman Foundation, Creation House, Inc., Illinois, 1971.

Ibid., I Corinthians, chapter 6, verses 19, 20, chapter 10, verse 13.

Ibid., II Corinthians, chapter 13, verse 14.

Ibid., Ephesians, chapter 1, verse 6, chapter 3, verse 16, chapter 5, verse 30.

Ibid., Hebrews, chapter 5, verse 14, chapter 12, verse 11.

Ibid., Isaiah, chapter 41, verse 10, chapter 55, verse 7.

Ibid., James, chapter 1, verses 2-5, 17.

Ibid., John, chapter 10, verse 27, chapter 14, verses 15-18, chapter 15, verse 14, chapter 16, verse 27.

Ibid., I John, chapter 1, verse 9, chapter 2, verse 2, chapter 4, verses 8-12.

Ibid., Matthew, chapter 13, verses 14, 15.

Ibid., I Peter, chapter 1, verses 6-9.

Ibid., Philippians, chapter 4, verse 13.

Ibid., Proverbs, chapter 1, verse 7, chapter 9, verse 10.

Ibid., Romans, chapter 5, verse 8, chapter 8, verses 1, 28, 31-34.

EPILOGUE

Kids are great. Isn't it wonderful that we adults can enjoy them?

More of them arrived today, and still more will be coming tomorrow. They grow up fast, scurrying around like a ragtail army, poking into odd places and shrieking with delight over the merest trifle. They are the same in any language, nationality, or culture—the lovable, immortal souls of children.

But some children are not as attractive as others. Youngsters with learning and behavior problems, for example, are difficult for most adults to love. Is it not, therefore, even more wonderful that professionally trained adults can fill this great void?

Specialties in education, psychology and medicine, along with those from the sub-divisions (or sub-specialties) of each discipline can combine the abilities and efforts of these disciplines to aid the child with learning and behavior problems.

Our goal is to correct as many problems as possible and to help these youngsters to adjust to what cannot be changed so they can live more normal lives.

This assistance can lead them from despair to joy. Their parents and close adult friends also reap the benefits of emotional stability in homes that are transformed and in classrooms that are calmed.

There is no single cure-all to these complex problems of human beings. Even though the proper use of medicine has afforded a major breakthrough by its ability to alter brain misfunction, medicines cannot bring a child automatically up-to-date on what was not learned in previous years. It does not magically produce success or even feelings of success at first. But it may improve function so that success is attainable. This results in properly earned success and brings the delightful feelings that normally accompany it. From good success comes good attention upon which we all should find it easy to build fruitful experiences.

It is of the utmost importance that each person in this fast-growing, rapidly expanding field keep an open mind to the new advances that improve the diagnosis, treatment and other phases of the condition. Yes, be open minded. But at the same time, don't let it become cluttered with the trash of unfounded bias. Be selective. Give due consideration to each item and profit from the pertinent. Don't be encumbered with meaningless material.

Some may ask why learning disabilities weren't a problem a decade or two or three ago. Are we reading too much into what really is quite normal? Why are there suddenly so many needing help.

The increase is due to:

1 · Greater population. *More people bring more problems.*

  —a relative increase

2 · The multiplication factor *due to the high hereditary genetic rate of the condition*

  —an absolute increase

3 · The toothpaste-tube principle

How do you get toothpaste out of the tube? You apply pressure and squeeze it out.

Individual, family, communal, city, state, national and international problems of all sorts are applying tremendous pressures on children today. The young are exposed to them much earlier in life than most of us adults were. They have most of their lives ahead of them. Many of us adults who counsel them have most of our lives behind us.

A realistic look at the world today is upsetting to many youngsters. They may not be able to give the details of the various critical issues but they can sense the pressures and tension that result from them. On the other hand, they may well know more about what is going on than we do because they are sharp. Remember: it's their world too!

When you add these external pressures, which are more frequent and of greater intensity than when we were young, the internal problems surface in full view—just like toothpaste, but not as orderly.

What better way is there to communicate with youth than to empathize with their all-important personal learning and behavior problems? We must accept and like each one as a person regardless of the type or the degree of his problems. We must work with and for him in methods that result in his gaining success, conquering his problems, and feeling accepted, worthwhile and competent as a happy, whole person.

CASE STUDY PROCEDURE CHECK LIST

NAME:_____

I.   Initial Referral form and the teacher's description forms
     forwarded to Pupil Personnel Services office.

                                        Date:_____

II. Psychologist reviews teacher description form and inter-
     views teacher, if clarification is needed.

                                        Date:_____

III. If teacher still desires study, psychologist observes pupil
     in classroom and school setting before any testing.

                                        Date:_____

IV. Psychologist administers tests as indicated.

                                        Date:_____

V.   Psychologist makes a verbal report of his (her) general
     impressions and plan of future action to the principal
     and teacher.

                                        Date:_____

VI. Psychologist conducts personal interview with parents and
     reports findings to them.

                                        Date:_____

VII. Psychologist requests any additional material from teacher,
     if needed.

                                        Date:_____

VIII. Psychologist reports total findings to principal and teacher
      and forwards written summary.

                                        Date:_____

IX. Psychologist forwards requests for further action to
     appropriate admissions committees or agencies as indicated.

                                        Date:_____

The psychologist is responsible to check (✔) each step as it is completed. A space has been provided for the date of action of this
would prove helpful.

This check list indicates the chronological procedures to be followed.

INITIAL REFERRAL FORM

School District

Special Services

Name _____ Sex _____ Birthdate _____ Phone _____

Parent-Guardian _____ Address _____

School _____ Grade _____ Session _____ Date _____

Referred By: _____

Reason for Referral: _____

_____ _____
(Date) (Principal)

Person Interviewed: _____

Findings and Recommendations: _____

_____

_____

_____

_____

_____ _____
(Date) Signature and Title

This form is used by the teacher and/or the principal in making the initial referral to the Special Education Department.

APPENDIX

_____ SCHOOL DISTRICT

TEACHER'S DESCRIPTION OF CHILD

Name:_____ BD:_____ Age:_____ Grade:_____ Sex:_____

School:_____ Teacher:_____ Room:_____ Date:_____

Please provide below your impressions of this child. Kindly check all
available records (cum, health, etc.) to supplement your observations. Include strengths as well as weaknesses.

Statement of Problem:

_____

_____

_____

_____

Mental Abilities:

Achievements in school:

Ability to communicate orally:

Physical and health factors:

Relations with other children:

Emotional behavior:

Interests:

Home factors:

Date parent contacted:_____ Date received in Dept._____

After the initial referral form has been submitted, the teacher sends more detailed information to the school psychologist on this confidential form.

(Physician's name and address)

DEAR PARENT:

PLEASE ASK YOUR CHILD'S TEACHER TO COMPLETE THIS FORM AND RETURN IT
TO MY OFFICE. PLEASE SIGN FORM IN THE SPACE DESIGNATED. THANK YOU.

Dear Teacher:

Please check one or more items listed below. The doctor needs your
view of the problem as he will be examining my child's learning and/
or behavior difficulties neurologically. Thank you.

Child's Name _____   _____
                                              Parents' Signature

ACHIEVEMENT
_____ Underachieving as you understand their ability

_____ Withdraws from reading   Actual classroom grade level

_____ Repeating the grade   in Reading _____

_____ Seems unable to concentrate   Spelling _____

_____ Poor follow through with work   Arithmetic _____

_____ Has short attention span

_____ Is easily distracted

BEHAVIOR   PHYSICAL FACTORS
_____ Temper tantrums   _____ Appears tired or sleepy

_____ Uncooperative   _____ Listless

_____ Nervous tic   _____ Eyes water, ache or blink
                                            from reading
_____ Irritable
                                _____ Cannot settle down after
_____ Over-active   exercise

_____ Restless or fidgety   Headaches: _____ anytime

_____ Plays by himself   _____ from reading

_____ Daydreams   _____ from exercise

_____ Withdrawn or depressed Stomachaches or upset:

                                           _____ from eating

                                           _____ from exercise

COMMENTS _____
_____
_____
_____
          Teacher's name   School

**This form provides initial information from the teacher about the child for
the physician. In private practice it is mailed to the parents ahead of their
visit so the teacher can complete it and have it returned to be available for
the initial office consultation and neurological examination.**

**In the school facility, the school nurse has the teacher complete this form
so it is available for the neurological examination at the school.**

_____ SCHOOL DISTRICT

Parent Questionnaire for School Doctor

Child's Name _____ Age _____

School _____ Date _____

PLEASE CHECK THE ITEMS LISTED BELOW AS THEY APPLY TO YOUR CHILD:

SLEEP HABITS

_____ Watching TV makes him sleepy

_____ Takes more than 30 minutes to go to sleep

_____ Restless while sleeping

_____ Deep sleeper

_____ Awakes during the night to go to the bathroom

_____ Awakens tired or irritable

_____ Has frequent nightmares

_____ Walks in his sleep

HEADACHES

My child has headaches: _____ frequently, _____ from reading,

_____ on awakening, _____ from playing.

STOMACHACHES

My child has a stomachache or nausea: _____ frequently, _____

from playing, _____ on awakening.

OTHER FACTORS

_____ Has had a bed wetting problem since kindergarten

_____ Bites his fingernails

_____ History of convulsions, seizures, fits or epilepsy from high fever, or head injury, or spontaneous

_____ History of convulsions, seizures, fits or epilepsy in family

COMMENTS: _____

_____

_____

Parent's Signature _____

The school nurse has the parent complete this form so it is available at the time of the child's neurological examination at school. This questionnaire is short, highlighting only pertinent information possibly related to the learning-behavior problem. The author insists that at least one parent be present during the neurological examination. For his office, an extensive, four-page questionnaire is filled out by the parents or guardian requesting detailed information regarding the family medical history and the past and present medical history of the child.

Teacher Follow-up Evaluation

Dear Teacher,   _____
                                                      date

    This pupil, _____ is on
                              (name)
medication. Your observations and comments regarding its effective-

ness or ineffectiveness, as pertaining to the following items, will

be most helpful and greatly appreciated.

    1. Attention span

    2. Concentration

    3. Distractibility

    4. Follow-through on work

    5. Activity - normal, over, or under active

    6. Fidgetiness

    7. Behavior - general or peer related

    8. Achievement in: Actual grade level:
        a) Reading   a) _____
        b) Spelling   b) _____
        c) Arithmetic   c) _____
        d) Other

    9. Handwriting, if a problem

    10. Mood swings

    11. Performance fluctuations

    12. Other

                            Thank you,

                            _____
                                      (signed)
                            (Name and address of
                             physician)

_____
        Teacher's Name

_____
Subject, if Jr.or Sr. H.S.

This form, explained in chapter 12, page 132, provides the physician with follow-up information from the teacher of the effects of medication. The parent is responsible for getting the form to the teacher and then back to the physician at each follow-up visit.

GLOSSARY*

Afferent Nerve   Any nerve that transmits impulses from the periphery (the body) toward the central nervous system (the brain and spinal cord).

Allergens   A substance which is capable of inducing allergy or specific susceptibility. Such a substance may be a protein or nonprotein.

Allergy   A hypersensitive state acquired through exposure to a particular allergen, re-exposure bringing to light an altered capacity to react which is not within normal limits.

Anemia   A reduction below normal in the number of erythrocytes per cu. mm., the quantity of hemoglobin.

Anxiety   A feeling of apprehension, uncertainty and fear.

Aphasia   Loss or impairment of the power to use words usually resulting from a brain lesion. Defect or loss of the power of expression by speech, writing or signs, or of comprehending spoken or written language due to injury, disease or other factors affecting the brain centers.

Apraxia, Motor   Loss of ability to make proper use of an object, although its proper nature is recognized.

Apraxia, Verbal   Inability to carry out purposeful speech in the absence of paralysis or other motor or sensory impairment, especially inability to make proper use of speech.

Ataxis   Failure of muscle coordination.

Attention Span   The length of time one can keep his mind on a given task.

Auditory   Pertaining to the sense of hearing.

Auditory Agnosia   Partial or total loss of the ability to recognize and/or interpret the stimuli received by the sense of hearing.

---

*The following dictionaries were used as resources:

Dorland's Illustrated Medical Dictionary, 24th edition. W.B. Saunders Company, Philadelphia, 1965.

The Manual of the Illinois Test for Psycholinguistic Ability (ITPA).

The Random House Dictionary of the English Language, the Unabridged Edition, Jess Stein, Editor-in-Chief, Random House, Inc., New York, 1967.

Webster's 7th New Collegiate Dictionary, G.&C. Merriam Co., Springfield, Massachusetts, 1963.

Auditory Closure   The ability to fill in missing parts which were deleted in auditory presentation and to produce a complete word.

Auditory Sequential Memory   The ability to reproduce from memory sequences of digits increasing in length from two to eight digits.

Audiovisual   Simultaneously stimulating, or pertaining to simultaneous stimulation of the senses of both hearing and sight.

Autistic, Autism   The condition of being dominated by subjective, self-centered trends of thought or behavior. Varying degrees of withdrawal from reality can be associated with this condition. There is no universally accepted definition at this time.

Autonomic   Self-controlling, functioning independently.

Autonomous   Characterized by autonomy, the state of functioning independently, without extraneous influence.

Biochemical   Biochemistry, the chemistry of living organisms and of vital processes; physiological chemistry.

Braille Method   Braille, a system of writing, printing or reading for the blind by means of tangible points or dots.

Cerebral   Pertaining to the cerebrum of which there are two: cerebrum—the large, main portion of the brain occupying the upper part of the cranium, the two cerebral hemispheres.

Cerebral Dysfunction   Disturbance, impairment, or abnormality of the functioning of the brain, particularly the two cerebral hemispheres, resulting in improper function of the body.

Cerebral Dysrhythmia   Disturbance or irregularity in the rhythm of the brain waves as recorded by electroencephalography.

Cluttering   Hurried nervous speech marked by the dropping of syllables; more than one sound, syllable or word competing to be spoken at the same time.

Cognition   The act or process of knowing, including both awareness and judgment.

Concept   The image of a thing (e.g. thought, notion) as held in the mind.

Convulsion   A violent involuntary contraction or series of contractions of the voluntary muscles.

Delusion   A false belief which cannot be corrected by reason.

Demyelinative Diseases Demyelinate—to destroy or remove the myelin sheath of a nerve or nerves.

Dexterity Readiness and grace in physical activity, skill and ease in using the hands.

Diadokokinesis, Diadokokinesia The function of arresting one motor impulse and substituting for it one that is diametrically opposite. Rapid alternating repetitive movements.

Directionality Pertains to the projection of right and left, up and down and other directions projected from the body out into the space about the body.

Dominance-Lateral The preferential use, in voluntary motor acts, of ipsilateral (situated on the same side) members of the major paired organs of the body (hand, ear, eye, foot).

Dysfunction Disturbance, impairment, or abnormality of the functioning of an organ.

Dysgraphia Inability to write properly because of ataxis, tremor, or motor neurosis.

Dyslexia The inability to read with understanding.

Dyssymbolia Failure of conceptual thinking so that thoughts cannot be intelligently formulated in language.

EEG Electroencephalogram: The graphic record obtained by electroencephalography which is the recording of the electric currents developed in the brain, by means of electrodes applied to the scalp. Brain wave test.

Efferent Nerve Any nerve that carries impulses from the central nervous system toward the periphery, i.e., away from the brain and spinal cord out to the body.

Empathy The capacity for participating in another's feelings or ideas.

Encephalitis Inflammation of the brain.

Encephalogram (see EEG).

Endocrine Pertaining to internal secretions. Applied to organs whose function is to secrete into the blood or lymph a substance (a hormone) that has a specific effect on another organ or part.

Environment Something that environs: surroundings. The complex of climatic and biotic factors that act upon an organism or an ecological community and ultimately determine its form and survival. The aggregate of social and cultural conditions that influence the life of an individual or community.

Epidemic Attacking many people in any region at the same time; widely diffused and rapidly spreading.

Epilepsy A disease characterized by one or more of the following symptoms: Paroxysmally recurring impairment or loss of consciousness. Involuntary excess or cessation of muscle movements, psychic or sensory disturbances, and perturbation of the autonomic nervous system. Symptoms are based on a substrate of paroxysmal disturbance of the electrical activity of the brain.

Etiology The study or theory of the causation of any disease; the sum of knowledge regarding causes.

Figure-Ground The singling out of a stimulus, be it visual, auditory or tactile, from surrounding similar or dissimilar stimuli.

Form-Constancy The ability to recognize or produce the same symbol, sign, design whenever desired.

Generic As related to medicine or drugs, it pertains to the chemical name of the substance.

Glandular Pertaining to or of the nature of a gland. Some use glandular as being synonymous with hormonal or endocrine.

Grammatic Closure The ability to make use of the redundancies of oral language in acquiring automatic habits for handling syntax and grammatic inflections.

Greed Excessive and inordinate desire.

Guilt The fact or state of having committed an offense, crime, violation or wrong, especially against moral or penal law—a feeling of responsibility or remorse from not being able to do what is correct or proper or being able to and yet not doing what is right.

Hate Intense hostility and diversion deriving from fear, anger or sense of injury; an habitual emotional attitude of distaste coupled with sustained ill will. A very strong dislike or antipathy. The opposite of love.

Hereditary Derived from ancestry or obtained by inheritance; in relation to disease, denoting a condition that may be genetically transmitted from parent to offspring.

Hormonal Pertaining to or of the nature of a hormone. A hormone is a chemical substance produced in the body, which has a specific effect on the activity of a certain organ.

Hostility, Hostile Marked by overt antagonism, unfriendly, resistant in thought and principle. The opposite of loving.

Hyperkinetic   Pertaining to hyperkinesia.

Hyperkinesia   Abnormally increased mobility; abnormally increased motor function or activity.

Hypokinetic   Abnormally diminished function or activity.

Impulsive   Actuated by or prone to act on impulse; acting momentarily.

Inorganic   Not of organic origin; being or composed of matter other than plant or animal; artificial.

Insight   The faculty of seeing into one's own inner character whether for the understanding of personal problems or for the normal feelings and attitudes of life.

Kinesthetic   The sense pertaining to the knowledge of the movements and position of muscles and the position of joints.

Learning Disability   The inability to learn at the level of one's ability.

Malice   Malevolence, ill will, spite, malignity, grudge.

Marasmus-Physical   Progressive wasting and emaciation, especially such a wasting in infants when there is no obvious or ascertainable cause. It can be related to inadequate intake of calories.

Maturational   Pertaining to the process of becoming mature or fully developed.

MBD   Minimal brain dysfunction.

Mental Retardation   These words give a poor description of what they are supposed to depict, and at the same time upset parents and those diagnosed as such. The dictionary defines them as experiencing an "absence of normal mental development." A better term is "Educational Retardation" or "Intellectual Retardation"—the latter defined as educational development below the average norm.

Metabolism, Metabolic   The sum of all the physical, chemical processes by which living organized substance is produced and maintained.

Monolithic   Characterized by massiveness, total uniformity, and intractability.

Mood Swings   Very rapid, fairly frequent and often unpredictable, change in feelings from happy to sad or from loving to hateful, or vice versa.

Morpheme   A meaningful linguistic unit whether a free form (as "pin") or a bound form (as the "s" of "pins") that contains no smaller meaningful parts.

Multidisciplinary   Multi means many, disciplinary—of or relating to a particular field of study.

NAS   New American Standard translation of the Holy Bible.

Nausea   An unpleasant sensation, vaguely referred to the epigastrium (upper portion of the stomach) and abdomen and often culminating in vomiting.

Neologisms   A new word, usage, or expression; a meaningless word coined by a psychotic.

Neo-natal Period   Pertaining to the first four weeks after birth.

Neurology, Neurological   That branch of medical science which deals with the nervous system, both normal and in disease.

Neuropathy   A general term denoting functional disturbance and/or pathological change in the peripheral nervous system. The etiology (cause) may be known or unknown.

Nystagmus   An involuntary rapid back and forth movement of the eyeball(s) which may be horizontal, vertical, rotatory, or mixed (two varieties).

Occipital   Pertaining to the occiput which is the back part of the head or the brain.

Ophthalmologist   An expert in ophthalmology.

Ophthalmology   The sum of knowledge concerning the eyes and their diseases.

Organic   Pertaining to substances derived from living organisms.

Otolaryngologist   A specialist in otology and laryngology. Otology is the sum of what is known regarding the ear. Laryngology is that branch of medicine which has to do with the throat, pharynx, larynx, nasopharynx and tracheo-bronchial tree.

Otologically   That which pertains to Otology (see Otolaryngologist).

Peer Pressure   Influence by others who are of the same age, rank or standing, or who have equal abilities or qualifications.

Permeability   Not impassable; pervious; that may be traversed. Penetrable.

Phoneme   The smallest units of speech that serve to distinguish one utterance from another in a language or dialect.

Phonics   Pertaining to the voice.

Phonetics   The science of vocal sounds.

Photic Stimulation   The specific usage here pertains to strobe light stimulation (at different frequencies) of the eye and brain with concurrent response being recorded on the EEG.

Physiologic   Normal; not pathologic (disease or injured); physiology—the science which treats of the functions of the living organism and its parts.

Placebo   An inactive substance or preparation, formerly given to please or gratify a patient, now also used in controlled studies to determine the efficacy of medicinal substances.

Prognosis   A forecast as to the probable result of any attack of disease or an abnormal condition in the body; the prospect as to recovery from a disease or condition as indicated by the nature and symptoms of the case.

Proprioception   The ability to receive stimulations within the tissues of the body. Proprioceptor—sensory nerve terminals which give information to the brain concerning movements and position of the body. Occurs chiefly in the muscles, tendons and labyrinth.

Psycholinguistics   The study of the relationships between language and the behavioral characteristics of those who use it.

Psychotic   One who has any major, severe form of mental disorder or disease, usually characterized by a withdrawal from reality.

® Registered Trade Mark   Which legally designates that it is reserved for the exclusive use of the owner as maker or seller.

Regression   Reversion to an earlier physical, mental or behavioral level. A trend or shift toward a lower or less perfect state.

Rejection   Action of rejecting; to refuse to acknowledge, hear, or consider; the act of refusing to accept someone.

Religion   The service and worship of God or the supernatural; a personal set or institutionalized system of religious attitudes, beliefs and practices.

Remediation   Curative, acting as a remedy.

Seizure   An attack of epilepsy.

Self-competence   The quality or feeling in one's self because he possesses and successfully uses his skill, knowledge, qualifications or capacities.

Self-image Concept   The image or feelings one has of himself in his own mind; how we see ourselves.

Sensory Agnosias   Loss of the power to recognize the import of sensory stimuli; the varieties correspond with the several senses and are distinguished as auditory, visual, olfactory (smell), gustatory (taste) and tactile (touch).

Side Effect   Usually refers to an undesirable effect produced by a medication that is in addition to its desired or proper therapeutic effect.

Somatic   Pertaining to or characteristic of the body (soma).

Sound Blending   The ability to synthesize the separate parts of a word and produce an integrated whole.

Sovereignty   Supreme and independent power or authority in governing.

Stammering   Speaking with involuntary breaks and pauses, or with spasmodic repetitions of syllables or sounds.

> *Stammer* more often implies a temporary inhibition through fear, embarrassment, or shock.

> *Stutter* suggests an habitual defect of speech organs or nerves but may imply a merely temporary effect of haste or excitement.

Stimulus (plural—stimuli)   Any agent, act or influence that produces a reaction (conscious or subconscious) in the body.

Strephosymbolia   (1) A disorder of perception in which objects seem reversed as in a mirror, (2) A reading difficulty inconsistent with a child's general intelligence, beginning with confusion between similar but oppositely oriented letters and a tendency to reverse direction in reading.

Stuttering   Speaking (words and sentences) in such a way that the rhythm is interrupted by repetitions, blocks or spasms, or prolongations of sounds or syllables, sometimes accompanied by contortions of the face and body.

Syndrome   A set of symptoms which occur together; the sum of signs of any morbid state. A symptom complex.

Tactile Perception   The conscious mental registration of a sensory stimulus received from the sense of touch.

Temporal   Pertaining to the lateral region of the head above the ear.

Trauma, Emotional   Shock that makes a lasting impression on the mind, especially upon the sub-conscious.

Trauma, Physical   A wound or injury.

Threshold   The point at which a physiological or psychological effect begins to be produced.

Trophic   Of or pertaining to nutrition; concerned in nutritive processes.

Underachievement . . . in Education   Performance that is not up to the level of one's academic ability in various areas (e.g., reading, spelling, arithmetic).

Understanding   Mental process of one who comprehends; skill in dealing with or handling something.

Vertigo   A sensation as if the external world were revolving around the patient or as if he himself were revolving in space (dizziness).

Visual   Pertaining to vision or sight.

Visual Acuity   Clearness of the vision as related to the optical function of the eyeball.

Visual Closure   The ability to identify a common object from an incomplete visual presentation.

Visual Discrimination   To distinguish accurately between two things with the sense of sight.

Visual Memory   Memory of visual impressions.

Visual Perception   The conscious mental registration of a sensory stimulus received from the sense of sight.

Visual Sequential Memory   The ability to reproduce sequences of nonmeaningful figures from memory.

Wisdom   Quality or state of being wise; knowledge of what is true or right coupled with just judgment as to action.

ABOUT THE AUTHOR

Robert D. Carpenter, M.D., is a general practitioner who has limited his practice for the past eight years to the neurological aspects of learning and associated behavior problems. His active patient load at present includes more than 500 cases, 87 per cent of whom are under 18 years of age.

His studies were undertaken at Wheaton College (B.S.) and Temple University School of Medicine (M.D.).

For the past two decades he has served for seven years as a medical missionary in the Taraja Congo Hospital, République du Zäire (formerly Congo), as physician and surgeon at the California Rehabilitation Center for Narcotic Addicts in Corona, and as a medical consultant for the Narramore Christian Foundation's Counseling Center at Rosemead, California.

The author has been in private practice at La Mirada, California, since August 1968, specializing in his chosen field.

He has served as school physician in the Special Education Program for seven elementary and junior high schools and for three high school districts. He is currently active in five elementary junior high districts and in two high school districts.

Over the past several years more than 900 neurological examinations for learning problems have been performed in these districts.

Licensed as a physician and surgeon in California, Washington and New Jersey, the author is a member of the Los Angeles County Medical Association, the California Medical Association, the American Medical Association and Christian Medical Missions.

ACKNOWLEDGEMENTS

A book is the work of many hands. I am indebted to my longsuffering wife, May, whose loving encouragement helped complete this editorial project. I am also in the debt of my office nurse, Mickey Morgan, to my secretary, Ann Stremski, and to Ruth Ewoldt for her initial editing of the burgeoning manuscript until Norman Rohrer ably prepared it for publication.

Other editorial cohorts include manuscript typist Joanne Blakey, and printer's consultant C. Leslie Miller whose indispensable expertise turned four years of work into a book.

Some of the reference material was supplied by William T. Whitney. His prowess as a reference librarian saved me untold hours of searching. His guidance and assistance in the preparation of the index was most helpful.

I have valued the personal association over the past eight years with Leon Oettinger Jr., M.D.—a nationally known leader in this specialty. I have appreciated his friendship and his help and have highly regarded his skill in the field of learning disabilities.

I appreciate also the knowledge shared in the interchange with personnel among the various school districts where I serve, with my colleagues in the medical, psychological and educational professions, and with others who have caught the exciting and growing challenge of helping those with learning and associated behavior problems.

Stuart E. Gothold, a school district superintendent, Clyde M. Narramore, a psychologist and director of a counseling center and graduate school of psychology, Barbara L. Nichols, a special education teacher for educationally handicapped minors, and F. S. "Jack" Warner, a pediatrician who treats the hyperkinetic syndrome child, read the entire manuscript. Glyndon Riley, a speech pathologist, reviewed the Speech and Hearing chapter. John and Lillian Seymour, parents of a neurologically handicapped pupil, reviewed the chapters pertaining to parents. All offered valuable help and advice. Their assistance is hereby gratefully acknowledged.

SUBJECT INDEX